Introducing Counselling and Psychotherapy Research

SAGE has been part of the global academic community since 1965, supporting high quality research and learning that transforms society and our understanding of individuals, groups, and cultures. SAGE is the independent, innovative, natural home for authors, editors and societies who share our commitment and passion for the social sciences.

Find out more at: **www.sagepublications.com**

Connect, Debate, Engage on Methodspace

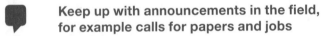 **Connect with other researchers and discuss your research interests**

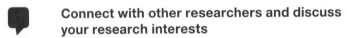 **Keep up with announcements in the field, for example calls for papers and jobs**

 **Discover and review resources**

 **Engage with featured content such as key articles, podcasts and videos**

 **Find out about relevant conferences and events**

www.methodspace.com

brought to you by

Introducing Counselling and Psychotherapy Research

Terry Hanley, Clare Lennie and William West

Los Angeles | London | New Delhi
Singapore | Washington DC

Los Angeles | London | New Delhi
Singapore | Washington DC

SAGE Publications Ltd
1 Oliver's Yard
55 City Road
London EC1Y 1SP

SAGE Publications Inc.
2455 Teller Road
Thousand Oaks, California 91320

SAGE Publications India Pvt Ltd
B 1/I 1 Mohan Cooperative Industrial Area
Mathura Road
New Delhi 110 044

SAGE Publications Asia-Pacific Pte Ltd
3 Church Street
#10-04 Samsung Hub
Singapore 049483

Editor: Alice Oven
Assistant editor: Kate Wharton
Production editor: Rachel Burrows
Marketing manager: Tamara Navaratnam
Cover design: Lisa Harper
Typeset by: C&M Digitals (P) Ltd, Chennai, India
Printed by MPG Books Group, Bodmin, Cornwall

Library of Congress Control Number: 2012937690

British Library Cataloguing in Publication data

A catalogue record for this book is available from
the British Library

MIX
Paper from
responsible sources
FSC
www.fsc.org   FSC® C018575

ISBN 978-1-84787-247-0
ISBN 978-1-84787-248-7 (pbk)

Terry – for Becky, Arthur, Matilda and Wilfred.

Clare – for Russ, and my beautiful sister Jane.

*William – for my friend Rev. Dr Chris Jenkins (1960–2011) and
for my father-in-law Peter Morton (1928–2004),
a farmer and gentleman.*

Contents

Figures, tables and graphs

Figure

Tables

Graphs

About the authors

Dr Terry Hanley is joint Programme Director of the Doctorate in Counselling Psychology at the University of Manchester and an experienced youth counsellor. He is an Associate Fellow of the British Psychological Society (BPS) and the Research Lead for the Division of Counselling Psychology (DCoP) within the same organisation. He has published widely in the field of youth counselling and is also the Editor of the DCoP's research publication *Counselling Psychology Review*. For his therapeutic practice he is registered in the United Kingdom by the Health and Care Professions Council (HCPC) as a counselling psychologist and is a British Psychological Society chartered psychologist.

Dr Clare Lennie is a chartered counselling psychologist and teacher. She works currently at the University of Manchester where she is joint Programme Director of the Doctorate in Counselling Psychology. Her research interests are around the positioning of counselling psychology in different organisational settings and related staff welfare, supervision and training issues. She has a particular interest in prison and oncology settings and the role that counselling psychology might offer there. In her past life she was a teacher of vocational and non-vocational courses in the sixth-form setting, before training in counselling to develop her pastoral skills and moving into student counselling and teacher training.

Dr William West is a Reader in Counselling Studies at the University of Manchester where most of his work is with PhD and Doctorate students. He is best known for his work around counselling and spirituality. He has a keen interest in postmodern research methods as applied to spirituality, culture, traditional healing and counsellor training and supervision. He is an accredited practitioner with the British Association of Counselling and Psychotherapy (BACP), former Chair of their Research Committee and is currently serving as past Chair of the Culture and Psychotherapy Special Interest Section of the Society for Psychotherapy Research (International).

1

Introduction

Abstract

This section provides a brief introduction to the text. It begins by introducing the rationale behind its conception and links this to the larger political moves to introduce research in therapeutic training programmes. Additionally, we introduce ourselves as the authors of the text. Here we attempt to provide some sense of our backgrounds and the wide variety of influences that inevitably impact upon the contents of this text. In the second half of this introductory chapter we focus upon the way in which the text has been written. In particular, we outline how the format of the book illustrates some of the research concepts that we talk about (e.g. this section is entitled abstract rather than overview), and we briefly outline some of the key terms that we use within the text.

> **THOUGHT BOX 1**
>
> **Why do you think a book like this is needed?**
>
> Consider:
>
> - Why did you pick it off the shelf?
> - What you might hope to get from it?
> - What might be your concerns of reading a research text?

The conception of the book: the personal becoming political

This book was conceived as much out of necessity as it was love for the subject matter. The three of us are fascinated by the world of counselling and psychotherapy research; however, we are very aware that not everyone shares our interest. As trainers, we have been involved in therapeutic training courses for numerous years and have observed a substantial change of emphasis upon what is deemed important within the counselling and psychotherapy training curriculum. In particular, since the turn of the century there has been a steadily increasing acknowledgement of the need for therapists to become research informed. The idea for this book therefore came out of these years of teaching and engaging with counselling students as they embark on a piece of research, or indeed elect not to embark on a piece of research! For the experiences of working with these groups we are exceptionally grateful.

As is noted above, the changing face of therapeutic training, and the role that research has within this, has led training institutions to redesign their courses to be in step with these new demands. The resulting need for counsellors to be research active leads to strong emotions and raises numerous tensions. For example, universities might value research endeavours more highly than practice and, due to the relative youth of counselling research, the associated places that such papers are published (i.e. in rather more practice-based journals) might be less prized for such institutions. Further, training teams may notice divides in their allegiance to practise or research activities. Given all of this, it is no wonder that trainees themselves are often polarised in terms of their feeling about continuing into research!

As trainers and trainees, we live the divide between the pursuits of research and practice and the external demands that are placed upon us. With this in mind, this book aims to capture the voices of trainees and trainers as we struggle with some of the issues around teaching and learning about research. Our hope is to bridge the divide in some small way and highlight the ways in which the two endeavours can complement one another. This is not to say that they are always the most natural of bedfellows, but we do feel that both can enrich each other's development.

So, who might be interested in reading this particular book? Our intention is to create something that has a potential currency for a wide variety of individuals. Without a doubt the obvious market would be those who are engaging in therapeutic training courses that have a research component; however, hopefully there will be others too. For instance, there may be individuals who completed therapeutic training courses prior to research becoming a major part of training and are therefore interested in continuing their professional development within this area; Doctorate students may want a refresher in particular areas; service managers may want to get a sense of what they might be doing to develop the evidence base for the work they support; and there may be those who just want an entertaining book for a beach holiday in Ibiza. OK, the last example may be a little far fetched, but we trust you get the picture.

The personal: the authors

Below we provide a brief introduction to ourselves and the voices that we bring to the text. Hopefully these voices will be clearly presented in what follows; where our voices are distinct in the text, these are identified with our initials. Having said this, it should however be noted that, despite the use of a primary voice in the chapters, each chapter is the end product of the thinking and writing of all three of the authors and we have each contributed to the content. We feel that, in pulling together a text such as this, it is important that we are transparent about the stances that we ourselves adopt. After all we are the lens through which much of what we present is filtered and, as with any piece of psychological research, we bring our own viewpoints and interests to this text. With this in mind, we not only ask you to be mindful of the potentially infinite alternative perspectives upon the subject matter that we present, but also briefly introduce ourselves below so that you have some sense of each of the backgrounds we bring to the work.

Terry (TH)

As a counselling psychologist I have a number of hats that link into this text. Below I discuss a few in no particular order.

I am a Lecturer in Counselling Psychology in higher education. This role means that I am actively involved in the training and researching of counselling and psychotherapy. As a trainer I provide input on counselling theory, research and practice, facilitate case discussion work and supervise research projects. Prior to this I have a background that took me from 24-hour care work, through youth work to counselling.

My therapeutic practice has predominantly been with young people within school, community and online settings. My practice is pluralist in nature (notably valuing whatever works for the individual sitting in front of me at that particular time) although it has a strong foundation within humanistic psychology. Given the context, it sounds trite to say that I am interested in research-informed approaches to therapy; however, this contrasts to the more commonplace model of research-directed therapy (do read on if this does not make sense to you at this point in time).

Within my research I have primarily concentrated upon therapeutic work with counselling services for young people. I whetted my appetite for this when I undertook an MA in Counselling and got trapped in a studying cycle that culminated in my completing a Doctorate in this area. This latter piece was a mixed methods study and ultimately led me to be fascinated in both the worlds of numbers and of words in research.

Outside of these professional hats it's difficult not to consider personal relationships with therapy. At the time of writing I have three children (Arthur, Matilda and Wilfred) and a dog called Mabel. Unfortunately I often think that I would not let some therapists I meet on my travels loose on Mabel, let alone myself or the precious baggage that often accompanies me. I do not anticipate that encouraging the therapeutic world to become more engaged with research will improve things overnight. I do however feel that it would be a useful starting point.

Clare (CL)

I am a teacher and counsellor and have worked at the University of Manchester as a Lecturer in Counselling Psychology since 2003. Prior to this I was a teacher for ten years in the sixth-form sector, teaching A Level and General Certificate in Secondary Education (GCSE) Psychology and health-related vocational courses to 16–19-year-olds. It was this work that triggered my interest in counselling as I became increasingly involved in student support and wanted to develop my skills in this area, hence my training as a counsellor. I have also worked on Postgraduate Certificate in Education (PGCE) programmes with trainee teachers. In my current post I work alongside Terry on the Doctorate in Counselling Psychology, and duties associated with this work centre on theoretical and research input, case discussion and thesis supervision. I see research as integral to our work as therapists.

Increasingly I have an interest in the different contexts in which counselling psychology and therapy find themselves. I describe myself as an integrative practitioner and my therapeutic background is predominantly with young adults. However, currently I am working in cancer care and forensic settings where we are developing links with our Doctorate in Counselling Psychology. As part of this work I am becoming increasingly interested in the emotional wellbeing of staff in complex and stressful work environments and the role that clinical supervision can offer to, for example, nurses and clinical staff in hospitals and residential wing staff in prisons.

When I am off duty from my university work, there is nothing I like better than wandering the world and exploring new places or hitting the gym to punch and kick the air. I live just outside of Manchester with my partner Russ and a baby grand piano.

William (WW)

I am Reader (Associate Professor) in Counselling Studies at the University of Manchester, where I am probably most noted for my research interest in counselling and spirituality and for my work with Doctorate and PhD students. I have a passion for postmodern qualitative research that (often) casts light on the human condition and consequently has value for practitioners. I feel that much good therapy remains a mystery encompassed by the therapeutic relationship and reckon that the best research gets closest to human experience. However, my life has been saved on two occasions by the National Health Service (NHS) using penicillin and surgery. This gives me great respect for quantitative methods and what they can deliver.

I have wrestled with the dilemma(s) around the role of the researcher in qualitative research for the last 20 years – played out in a number of research studies in which I have used grounded theory, thematic analysis and heuristics. With a great suspicion of ideology and hero worship, I take a pragmatic view of research methods choice, focusing on what gets the job done efficiently and hopefully elegantly. I also have a keen interest in rhetoric that leads to the question of how effectively to disseminate research findings.

I have written: two authored books – *Psychotherapy and Spirituality* (Sage 2000), *Spiritual Issues in Therapy* (Palgrave 2004); one edited book – *Exploring Therapy, Spirituality and Healing* (Palgrave 2011); and one co-edited book with Roy Moodley,

Integrating Traditional Healing Practices into Counseling and Psychotherapy (Sage 2005); 28 peer-reviewed papers, 16 book chapters and 29 papers in professional journals. I am a past Chair of the Culture and Psychotherapy Special Interest section of the Society for Psychotherapy Research (International), Fellow of the BACP and former Chair of their Research Committee.

I am a keen cyclist, amateur poet and beginner piano player.

The trainees

Co-authors on this project have been those people who have conscientiously read through our chapters and very kindly put together a response to our words. These individuals have all endured and, we hope, at times enjoyed the research training that we are involved in delivering at the University of Manchester. They come from a wide variety of therapeutic practice backgrounds and have been involved in our MA in Counselling and Doctorate in Counselling Psychology programmes.

Writing style

A major aim of this text is to produce something that is informative and accessible to a wide array of readers. Although we hope the text will challenge you in parts, if the messages that we are trying to get across are not clear, then we haven't achieved one of our goals. Each chapter therefore takes a main theme and presents some of the dilemmas that have come across from the work we have undertaken with trainees. We have attempted to write about these ideas in a language that enables individuals to engage with the topic at the same time as introducing some of what we consider to be important pieces of literature.

Research language can often be daunting and difficult to get your head around. Linked to the point above, it can also be one of the major factors that turn people off reading research. Within the chapters that follow, we do not shy away from using research terms, but we purposefully do not jump into the deep end. Additionally, we attempt to utilise some of the key terms that you might find in research papers within the chapters themselves. For instance, at the start of this chapter we had an abstract, which is essentially a summary of the chapter (literally an 'abstraction' of its key points). Throughout the chapters we will present you with a number of activities to generate your own 'findings' before getting you to reflect upon them in a 'discussion' section. Once again these are sections that you will find in most research papers and hopefully their purpose will become a little clearer as you read on.

As trainers who work within a department that offers professional training programmes at Masters and Doctorate levels in several therapeutic disciplines (counselling, counselling psychology and educational psychology), it has been important for us to devise input directly relevant to the trainees who attend these courses. Here we would note that it may have been possible to offer trainees an amalgamation of 'off the peg' sessions from colleagues around the university solely focusing upon research methods. However, such a solution, although potentially proving desirable by institutions that are inevitably interested in saving money, seemed far from satisfactory for the trainees that we were working with. Specifically, it seems important that when attempting to engage professionals in research discussions, the examples have some resonance to their practice. Without this, we feel we may end up falling at the first hurdle.

As noted above, we hope that the text is not a dry read and combines informed content (presented in a palatable way) with reflective activities that encourage you to consider the impact of the subject matter upon yourself. The activities presented reflect the training material that we use within the courses we teach on and have been tailored for individual use. We hope that these give you a chance to reflect personally upon the content of the text and also to compare your views with those of others. We also hope that they prove useful and enjoyable.

The final comment in each chapter comes from individuals who have trained with us. We ask them to give an alternative perspective upon the content we have provided. Here we hope to achieve several things:

1) Pluralism: First we would acknowledge that it is not possible to present everything related to a subject within the parameters of a single book chapter. Furthermore, others may have vastly differing but relevant views on the content provided. Contributors to this 'member checking' section will therefore be able to reflect upon areas that we have not presented within the text.

2) Utility: Linked to the first point, we also ask contributors to highlight sections they perceive to be strengths of the chapter and outline important elements that may have been missed within the content. More specifically, contributions have been sought to reflect explicitly upon those bits that are useful and those that are less useful.

3) Member check: Finally, the purpose of this section provides an opportunity to reflect upon some of the findings that are presented within the work. Within qualitative research (e.g. a project that interviewed people) a member check relates to a process in which you might share your conceptualisation of the interview with the person who took part to check that you are making use of their contributions appropriately. Here trainees have been provided with the opportunity to reflect upon our presentations with a view to presenting alternative or additional views. Within this book we have decided to present the member checks alongside the content that we have created, rather than amend it following them. It is hoped that such a presentation will display some of the dialogic nature of the content within the chapter and reflect the richness in these discussions – particularly noting that the presentations we provide are but a starting point from which the interested reader may follow up numerous leads.

In the interests of transparency, and for the interested reader, the instructions for the member check activity were given as follows.

ACTIVITY BOX 1

Critique a book chapter

Please read through the book chapter that we have created and consider the following:

- What are your responses to the chapter?
- What are its strengths and weaknesses?
- Are there bits you would have liked to be included?
- Are there bits you would have developed? Etc.

When you have considered these questions, can you organise these responses into (approximately 4) themes? Can you then bring these together into approximately 4 paragraphs of about 250 words each? Total word count = 1000 words.

THANK YOU!

You may want to complete a similar activity on completion of reading sections of the book for your own learning process. As you will see from the contributions, some individuals stayed truer to the task than others but all offer an alternative angle on the content.

Finally, at the end of each chapter, we will suggest potential extension reading for those who wish to follow up leads presented in the text. The sources noted here we hope will signpost readers to good-quality material that will develop further the readers' understanding of the topics. However, for those of you who have had enough (for now), we hope that the core chapter will be sufficient to give you a grounding for each of the topics under consideration.

Defining key terms

In texts such as this, or research projects, it is always helpful to begin with a brief overview of key terms that may prove confusing. The terms that need some brief attention within the text are 'counselling' and 'psychotherapy' and 'research'.

Counselling and psychotherapy

For many the terms 'counselling' and 'psychotherapy' mean something completely different. Within this text, however, we are viewing them as terms that reflect a broad skill set that has numerous overlapping components. Alongside this we would accompany these terms with therapeutic language such as 'therapy' and protected titles such as 'counselling psychologist' and 'clinical psychologist' – although we choose not to use the latter so as not to cause confusion. This decision is in part research informed as there is very little research noting differences in the practice of individuals adopting the different titles. In essence, this means that within this text the terms 'counselling', 'psychotherapy' and 'therapy' are used interchangeably throughout.

Research

This is a curious term to attempt to define. It has particular nuances and uses that prove confusing and unhelpful at times. However, rather that attempting to address such issues here, fortunately Chapter 3 pays substantial attention to the notion of 'What is research?'

The structure of the book

As is obligatory in textbooks of this kind, it is usual to provide a brief synopsis of what follows within the introductory chapter. Now this text does not attempt to do anything different; however, as it focuses upon research, which is often presented in rather long documents, it feels appropriate to mention briefly why this is the case before doing so. Thus, including a short roadmap of the territory that is to be covered by the sections/ chapters that follow helps to guide the reader through the text. Content of this kind can therefore help to sensitise the reader to what is going to come up and remind them of where they have been. Now for the content.

Chapters 2 and 3 begin with a rather political slant. Chapter 2 aims to get people thinking by discussing the research that underpins therapeutic work. Importantly we get into the territory of 'Does therapy actually work?' After all, does it? We may think that it does, and key psychologists we admire may tell us that it does, but is this actually true? For those of you who do not know about the important part the dodo plays in the development of counselling and psychotherapy practice, this chapter is definitely for you. In Chapter 3 we then answer the simple question of 'What is research?' For some, the term may be held aloft by an elite bunch of people just like a sporting trophy. For others, deference may turn into petrifaction and fear. This chapter aims to demystify the notion of research and present some commonalities within all research projects. Alongside this we hope to convey the notion that we are all undertaking research activities every day – it really is that simple.

In the next two chapters we consider issues that individuals might want to reflect upon prior to undertaking a project and the potential consequences that might be bestowed on an individual whilst they are doing it. Chapter 4 begins by reflecting upon the considerations that individuals have whilst preparing to undertake a project. In particular, we outline the importance of developing a critical stance within any piece of research and also highlight the importance of passion. These facets will not ensure the success of a project, but they will go a long way to creating something meaningful. Following on from this, Chapter 5 introduces the potential impact of undertaking a piece of research on the researcher. Here we consider the motivations behind the scenes of research projects and the hurdles that individuals might encounter during the lifespan of a research project. Be warned, it will not be easy sailing. There is, however, help on hand.

In the next three chapters we get a little more applied and consider issues related to *doing* research. Chapters 6 and 7 reflect in turn on quantitative research (research primarily using numbers) and qualitative research (research primarily using words) in counselling and psychotherapy. Both of these chapters introduce the reasons for utilising very different research methods. Additionally, they provide brief overviews of what to look for in good-quality research of these types. Chapter 8 then reflects upon the important issue of ethical soundness within research. Just as therapists have to work to certain standards within their therapeutic practice, similar values need to be adhered to when conducting research. This chapter outlines a number of key issues, such as what can and can't be done in the name of research, and who undertakes ethical review of research projects.

Chapter 9, the final chapter before our summing-up in Chapter 10, ends by reflecting upon the ways in which people talk about research. Research needs to be communicated to interested others, otherwise it is likely to sit on a supervisor's shelf and gather dust. This chapter therefore discusses potential outlets for counselling and psychotherapy research and outlines some of the major concerns that people have when considering sending their work off into the wider community.

(In the words of Columbo) Just one more thing …

Before moving on to the main event, we would encourage you to undertake one final activity. Before reading any further, contemplate what you hope to get from reading the text. With this in mind, we ask you to consider the following questions:

1 What are your goals when reading this text?
2 How good do you think your knowledge of research issues is? (Before getting into the main chapters of this book.)

Activity Box 2 provides instructions for reflecting upon these two questions. Initially you are asked to identify your goals in reading the book before completing what we have titled SARA, our Self-Assessed Research Awareness questionnaire, version 1.

ACTIVITY BOX 2

Identify your goals and initial research literacy

What are your goals?

Identify 3–5 goals that you have in reading this text. Note these down and keep them in a safe place – e.g. a research journal.

(Continued)

(Continued)

How research literate are you?

The SARA questionnaire

Rate your knowledge of each topic noted below on a scale of 0–5 (0 = I know nothing about this, 5 = I am very aware of this issue).

- The research that underpins therapy
- What is the purpose of research?
- The issues related to preparing to undertake research
- The impact that research has upon the researcher
- Quantitative research
- Qualitative research
- The ethical issues within therapy research
- The arenas in which counselling and psychotherapy research is talked about

Please note SARA v.1 is a playful tool devised solely for illustrative purposes – although it could potentially develop into an interesting research project. We will revisit it as the text progresses – especially in Chapters 6 and 10 – so do keep a note of your answers handy.

2

The Research Underpinning Therapy: Does Therapy Really Work?

Abstract

We now enter the main event of this text. As the title of this chapter suggests, we will explore some pretty important territory for the world of counselling and psychotherapy, notably 'Does therapy really work?' (a question that is never going to be as straightforward as may be hoped). In doing so we will begin by reflecting upon which therapeutic approach works best. Initially, a brief consideration of the complexities inherent in this question is provided before reflecting upon the arguments for and against therapy. We then move on to describe the historical context for research into counselling and psychotherapy and look at the types of evidence utilised to justify the work that therapists undertake with clients. These discussions help us to consider the amount of research that supports therapeutic practice and to question how well counsellors utilise it to support their work. Finally, Nadim Siddiqui, one of our present students and an experienced cognitive-behavioural therapist, is then let loose to reflect upon the chapter as a whole, and a number of excellent resources are recommended for those hoping to follow up the content of this chapter.

THOUGHT BOX 2

Which approach to therapy works best?

Consider:

- What answer would you give?
- What evidence would you refer to when backing up your claim?
- What weaknesses would there be in your argument?

Which approach to therapy works best?

Clearly the answer to the question posed in Thought Box 2 is cognitive-behavioural therapy (CBT). Before you feel the desire to write and complain about our broad-brush sweeping statement, we ask you to think why you agree or disagree with it. Presently it is a viewpoint that is often mooted around the therapeutic world, and it is also one in which there is at least *some* truth (truth is an issue that we will return to in later chapters). However, just to clarify, although the approach is clearly of benefit to a great number of people it will not be of use to everyone – a view that we link directly to the literature regarding therapeutic outcomes in the second half of this chapter. So, how would you evaluate the claim? And if you felt to the contrary, how would you defend the approach of therapy that you practise?

Let's begin by considering in more detail the claim, 'cognitive-behavioural therapy is the best therapy'. Straight away we can outline limitations in this statement and consider:

1   What exactly do we mean by 'CBT'?
2   What do we mean when we use the term 'best'?

and

3   Who are we claiming that it works 'best' for?

Each one of these facets can considerably change what the statement means and we'll briefly discuss each one in turn.

1 What exactly do we mean by 'CBT'?

The term CBT can refer to an incredibly wide variety of therapeutic approaches (e.g. Mansell and Taylor, 2012). Practitioners may work in a way that emphasises the 'cognitive' element or the 'behavioural' element, or they may feel they inhabit worlds aligned to first-, second- or third-wave approaches (e.g. see Mansell, 2008). Furthermore the person offering therapy may have been trained in a very different manner. We are presently seeing an influx of people offering CBT who have completed a short training programme and may have no other therapeutic training. Likewise, computerised versions are becoming big business and forging a place in our mental health care systems. However, is the CBT offered by a computer, or an individual who has only completed a short training programme, different from that offered by a counsellor or clinical psychologist? The likelihood is yes, but how these differ, and whether one is more effective than the other, is another matter.

A new development in the world of therapy is the outlining of core competencies for practitioners (e.g. if we stick with CBT for the time being, see Roth and Pilling, 2007). These aim to tighten up the ways in which therapeutic models are taught, practised and supervised. As a consequence, these guidelines may help to clarify what is meant when individuals claim to work with a specific approach in mind. Such an approach fits more congruently with therapeutic approaches that place an emphasis upon specific skills;

however, core competencies for humanistic and psychodynamic approaches of therapy have also been created (see Roth, Hill and Pilling, 2009, and Lemma, Roth and Pilling, 2008, respectively). Only time will tell if such an approach makes therapy more consistent in the way that it is applied.

2 What do we mean when we use the term 'best'?

I am sure that I am the 'best' therapist in the world. Now, this may be true, but how would I prove it? And what does the term 'best' actually mean? Two issues that often come into play when considering this topic are clinical effectiveness and cost effectiveness. The former is probably the most commonplace with practitioners. Counsellors are familiar with the notion of having to prove their worth in terms of making people feel better when they access the services that they offer. The latter often falls into the realms of service managers. These individuals don't just have to justify the worth of services to funding bodies and commissioners, they have to do so in a highly competitive marketplace. For instance, other services advocating brief therapy may promise the same outcomes over a shorter period of time and thus at a cheaper cost. Such realms are not for the faint hearted and, worryingly, counselling services have been slow to respond.

And finally …

3 Who are we claiming that it is 'best' for?

When considering the scientifically minded way in which mental health care is presently allocated within UK-based statutory services, this question proves incredibly pertinent. It is often muted that CBT is viewed as the panacea to all our psychological problems; however, even within NICE (the National Institute for Health and Clinical Excellence) guidelines this is not the case. True, CBT does factor highly, but there are other recommended responses for specific difficulties. For instance, alternative models such as cognitive-analytic therapy, psychodynamic psychotherapy and family therapy are presently recommended for the treatment of people with a diagnosis of anorexia nervosa. Thus, the world that advocates evidence-based practice (also referred to as empirically supported treatments) does acknowledge the importance of other models of therapy.

On another note, when considering who therapy is 'best' for, we question the social role that counselling and psychotherapy plays. Do research findings indicate that therapy is beneficial for the client, the service offering therapy or society itself? As practitioners, my guess is that we would like to think the former comes first; however, the others are always present. We will return to these issues in Chapter 5 of this book.

Without a doubt, assessing which approach to therapy works best is a complex matter. There are numerous questions to be asked regarding the foundation of these issues, and some of these will be further unpacked later on in this text. Here, however, we hope to give a flavour of a world that is far from straightforward. In the activity that follows we refer directly to the experiences of counsellors who are in training. How do they perceive the debates that rage about the effectiveness of therapy?

ACTIVITY 3: The great psychotherapy debate

A commonplace feature of our counsellor training is 'the debate'. This has an additional relevance to this topic as the American writer Bruce Wampold has written an incredibly thought-provoking text called *The Great Psychotherapy Debate* which enters this territory (Wampold, 2001b; this is a great text, but does cover some pretty complicated issues). Within our training courses it is easy to get passions riled and generate interesting discussions by getting trainees to argue with each other about which approach of therapy is best. They are asked to split into groups and encouraged to think about the evidence base for different counselling approaches (e.g. Group one – person-centred, Group two – psychodynamic and Group 3 – cognitive-behavioural). Then they are asked to present a case of support for their allocated therapy before the whole group decides which therapy has presented the most compelling debate. This element is further linked into practice issues by asking the group to decide which therapy they would commission based on the evidence provided. Now we can't ask you to split yourself in half and debate in this way, but we can encourage you to consider the evidence base for your own practice. In the activity below we therefore ask you to consider the defence you would put forward for your own practice.

This activity attempts to:

1 encourage the reader to consider the evidence base for their practice
2 support the reader in reflecting upon the strengths and weaknesses in the evidence utilised to support their practice

and

3 encourage the reader to reflect upon the place research has when commissioning bodies decide upon what services to fund.

The activity

This is an activity to undertake with no preparation or resources to hand. Imagine being caught on the hop by a professional colleague. For instance, a teacher in the school you are working in as a counsellor, or similarly a GP in a surgery, asks you as you pass in a corridor,

'What approach of therapy do you use?'

and follows it up with,

'What evidence is there that it works?'

before finally asking,

'Does that fit with NICE guidelines?'

Such questioning would prove commonsense in many professions, but historically this hasn't been at the forefront of counsellors' minds. With that in mind, we ask you quickly to note down the evidence for your therapeutic approach of choice. What will you use to impress your colleague? And what might you leave out? Just to remind you, the task is outlined in Activity Box 3.

Following on from having to make your case whilst in a hurry, we now want you to look at what you have produced and change the scenario you are confronted with. Now we want you to consider that the teacher or GP is firmly in charge of the purse strings of the organisation. They are trying to decide whether or not to recommission the work that you do for them. We recognise that you would have more time in the real world to present your case, but how well do you think you would fare? Would your service get recommissioned? Would there be any holes in your arguments that the commissioner might want to ask about? And finally, how might your argument be improved?

ACTIVITY BOX 3

The great psychotherapy debate

Create a case to defend the approach of therapy you adopt.

Part 1

Consider:

- What evidence you would use to defend your therapeutic approach. (What might you also omit?)

Part 2

Consider:

- If you were a service commissioner, would you be convinced by your argument? What questions might you have?
- How might you develop your defence in the future?

Your findings

Now let's say that your job is on the line here – no pressure! Do you feel that you've done a good enough job defending your practice? If you are confident in the argument then that's great. If not, then maybe it's time to revisit the textbooks and journal databases to support the work that you enter into. For a strong argument we would hope to see you develop your case using high-quality source material. This would include having a sound theoretical foundation alongside up-to-date research. Did you do this? In fact, do you know of any research articles that support the theoretical position that you adopt as a counsellor? Some counsellors and psychotherapists are very sketchy when it comes to this. It may also be that you have to defend the quality of the research you cite. Do you know whether the journals the articles are published in are any good? This may seem snobbish, but there are clear hierarchies of journals. Furthermore, the place in these hierarchies will reflect the status and subsequent power of its contents. For instance, a professional journal such as the BACP's *Therapy Today* is a lot less authoritative than an article published in the same organisation's research journal *Counselling and Psychotherapy Research* (*CPR*). Following on from this, *CPR* is eclipsed by numerous other higher-status publications.

The next question asks you to consider whether your service would get commissioned based upon your argument. In addition to scrutinising the quality of evidence you have provided, the commissioner will also have the arguments posed by other groups. Do you feel your argument would put you on top of the pile and get selected? In every argument there are flaws, or other ways of looking at the evidence provided. Thus, with this in mind, what audience have you aimed for? For instance, the NHS will have a different view than charitable bodies in some instances. How possible would it be to strengthen your case for a different audience? Needless to say, asking questions such as these can raise issues that cut to the heart of therapy. There is no definitive answer, but there are stronger arguments.

Our findings

In this section we reflect upon the types of arguments that trainees provide when answering these questions. As noted above, this is undertaken in a number of groups, with each group being encouraged to create the most compelling debate to defend an approach of therapy. At the end of the debate a vote is taken to see which argument is viewed as the strongest, and thus becomes the commissioned service. This proves a very energetic activity that raises lots of important questions about what makes 'good' therapy.

In presenting the findings from the groups we do not intend to reflect upon the different therapeutic approaches one by one (e.g. psychodynamic therapy can be viewed most beneficial because …). Instead we will present a few pertinent issues that always arise. These are clinical effectiveness, cost effectiveness and client choice. These we will mention in turn.

Clinical effectiveness

As controversial as the assessment of clinical effectiveness can be, most people agree that it is an important issue for therapists. With this in mind, there are an abundance of sources supporting work from all therapeutic paradigms. These can vary greatly in form and can range from large-scale outcome studies to individual case studies. Trainees are commonly aware of a small number of research projects but generally knowledge is relatively sparse – understandably so, as most trainees are grappling with the complexities of the psychological theory itself. There is also an awareness that NICE guidelines often advocate the use of CBT, but once again the substance behind this is sometimes a little lacking (e.g. why do NICE support CBT for certain issues?). Additionally, there is often confusion of how to use smaller-scale evidence, such as case studies and personal reflections on practice, to support their practice. Individuals are commonly influenced greatly by such work, want to include it somewhere, but are also mindful that it can be easily criticised for the limited number of people involved. To end, we must also not forget that, although we have reflected the weaknesses of many trainees' arguments here, some are incredibly well versed in arguing their case. Many a time a student has brought to our attention a fascinating piece of work that provides yet another view of the effectiveness of a particular therapeutic approach.

Cost effectiveness

This one is always a favourite issue to raise in the debates. It is commonly introduced by those supporting therapies such as CBT because of the way they fit into the schema for brief therapies. Stringent timescales can be placed on interventions and therefore be argued to be a cheaper option – less input by a therapist being deemed as less financial outlay by an employer. This also feeds into the idea that cheaper services can support more clients, thus increasing access to psychological therapies. However, there are always counterpoints to such an argument. For instance, CBT is not always short term, and time-limited person-centred and psychodynamic services do exist and have shown themselves to be beneficial. Also, if cost is the major factor, how do we account for the multitude of counsellors working as volunteers? Furthermore, there is always the sticky plaster argument, with some therapists arguing that certain short interventions may be akin to plugging a dam with your finger – notably they will work in the short term, but the dam is likely to leak again at some point in the future. Unfortunately, what our students highlight is that money doesn't just make the world go round, it also greatly influences the commissioning of therapeutic services.

Client choice

Once again we hit a fascinating issue that proves incredibly controversial. This is a vastly under-researched area and one that receives a great deal of lip service in policy documents. The argument is often mooted in the groups that clients want the service that they provide and they have made an informed choice to use it. Such information is gathered from sources such as discussions prior to therapy and vindicated by responses to feedback questionnaires at the end of therapy. However, some students playfully raise the questions: Is this really a strong argument? Can clients truly make an informed judgement? Is the decision better made by an informed professional? And, what happens if a client chooses something that isn't available? Or is too costly? Or is unsupported by the existing body of evidence? And so on. The debate goes on and returns to the question of clinical effectiveness.

Making a decision

So which therapy is chosen by the students to be funded? Invariably this is a difficult decision and we will stay on the fence here and just note that the answer varies. Importantly, while making a decision the above issues are all contemplated and the complexity of such a choice made very real.

Discussion

Within our classes we have found this exercise to be both lively and thought provoking. The trainees we have worked with have commonly entered into the spirit of the debate and played along with our prods to become competitive. With this in mind, the playful nature of the task makes it an enjoyable activity that evokes a number of important issues. For instance, some of the issues that arise naturally whilst undertaking this activity include discussions around the clinical and cost effectiveness of different therapeutic approaches, and the nature of 'evidence'. You may have noticed similar issues in your own thinking? Therefore, this activity brings to life politically sensitive issues within the counselling profession. This is no more evident than when considering whether an approach should be commissioned or not!

   This activity acts as a starting point for many of the exercises presented in this text. It attempts playfully to get individuals to reflect upon the political challenges that counselling services face on a day-to-day basis. It should also confront readers with the knowledge that their therapeutic approach of preference is not without fault. Whether it is the lack of hard-nosed outcome research or the limited connection to everyday practice, no therapy consistently comes out on top, and the judgements that are made are done so from within a specific view of the world. For us, as tutors, this becomes a rich tapestry of intrigue. However, we must not forget that, to others (e.g. possibly the readers of this book and our students), it's a potential professional livelihood that can become increasingly confusing and a frustrating mystery.

Does therapy work? And if so, which works best?
A very brief overview

As is noted in the Introduction to this book, research within the world of counselling and psychotherapy has steadily developed and increased in importance in recent years. This is not to say that it's a new phenomenon. Far from it in fact – at the very conception of psychotherapy the case-study approach of research proved incredibly popular. However, such methods, which were taken as gospel by early psychotherapists such as Freud and his adversaries, were vehemently challenged by Hans Eysenck during the early 1950s (Eysenck, 1952) and acted as a pivotal point in the great psychotherapy debate. In his review of 24 research studies Eysenck concluded that there was no evidence to suggest

Table 1 A summary of the four generations of counselling research

Generation	Years	Focus of research
1	1950s–1970s	Is psychotherapy effective? Are there objective methods for evaluating therapy?
2	1960s–1980s	Which approach of therapy is most effective? What components of therapy are related to better outcomes?
3	1970s–1990s	How can therapy be made more cost effective? How does change occur?
4	1980s ongoing	Does therapy produce clinically significant change? What are the effective ingredients of therapy?

Source: Based upon Barkham, 2003: 25–73.

that attending therapy was any more effective than not attending therapy. Although this view has been challenged greatly since it was first published it is a view that changed the mindset of the profession. No longer can it rest on its laurels and assume that it has a rightful place in health care provision.

Following Eysenck's criticism the focus of research within this arena has gone through a number of phases. Barkham (2003) describes four different generations of research into therapy. Table 1 summarises these different generations by outlining the dates in question and the key questions that were posed.

Throughout this period significant progress has been made and many now claim that the general effectiveness of therapy has been convincingly demonstrated (Lambert and Bergin, 1994). One of the first major studies that helped to establish the efficacy of therapy was that conducted by Smith and Glass (1977). This meta-analysis (an approach of amalgamating studies for larger impact) of 475 trials compared treatment with no treatment over 18 therapeutic approaches. In doing so they found that the average person who attended therapy was more likely to be better off than 80 per cent of those who did not.

So, if therapy is likely to benefit individuals in need of emotional support, we return to the question, which approach works best? After over fifty years of research the answer appears to be none of them. Research has convincingly displayed all approaches to produce equivalent outcomes, a factor that Luborsky, Singer and Luborsky (1975) describe as the 'dodo bird verdict' (a term originally used as far back as 1936 by Rosenzweig). This refers to the caucus race in Lewis Carroll's *Alice in Wonderland* in which the dodo bird proclaims at the end of the event that 'All have won and all shall have prizes'. The implication of such a finding proves significant within the world of counselling and psychotherapy as it challenges the notion that specific therapeutic approaches can be classified as more effective than others, a view that becomes ever-more pertinent within the UK as the rhetoric behind cognitive-behavioural approaches to therapy become increasingly dominant. Bergin and Garfield note:

One of the most difficult findings to conceptualise theoretically or to use practically is the continuing and frequent lack of difference in outcomes of various techniques. With some exceptions … there is massive evidence that psychotherapeutic techniques do not have specific effects, yet there is tremendous resistance to accepting this finding as a legitimate one. (1994: 822).

The combination of this equivalent outcome finding and professional resistance has led individuals to challenge the view that services can be appropriately commissioned based upon research into specific therapeutic schools (see for example, Wampold, 2001b; Lambert, 2004; and Westen, Novotny and Thompson-Brenner, 2004 for compelling debates). The validity of the concept of empirically supported treatments therefore becomes much hazier due to the lack of clarity about what variables are actually impacting upon the outcome of therapy.

In more recent years, within Barkham's fourth generation of therapeutic research, a number of theoreticians and researchers have begun to ask the question 'What are the important ingredients of successful therapy?' rather than 'Which approach of therapy is best?' This stance is often described as a common factors approach and has produced some thought-provoking findings for the profession. The common factors approach quite often gets linked to the emergence of integrative and eclectic practices of therapy (see for example, Hollanders, 2000). Its origins date back to the inter-war period within the twentieth century with individuals such as French (1933) and Rosenzweig (1936) attempting to create dialogues between the deeply entrenched behaviourist and psychoanalytic practitioners. In a similar vein Watson (1940) initiated a number of discussions between practitioners from the different schools of thought. His conclusions from this work note that agreement between therapists was 'greater in practice than in theory' (1940: 708).

The work exploring common therapeutic factors has continued to develop and gather pace since Watson's work in 1940. Numerous theories have emerged outlining different takes on the common factors in question. For instance, Frank (1961) highlighted the importance of 'emotional arousal', 'increased self-esteem', 'increased hope', 'different views of the problem' and 'a focused activity to engage in', as key influences in therapeutic change. Also Karasu (1986), after identifying over 400 different schools of therapy, noted 'affective experiencing', 'cognitive mastery' and 'behavioural reformulation' to be common elements in each approach. Thus, almost ironically the formulations of the common factors theories have themselves become increasingly varied.

In recent years one of the most cited explorations of common factors has been offered by Lambert and his colleagues (Asay and Lambert, 2000; Lambert and Barley, 2002). Within their reviews of the outcome literature they identify four main factors that influence progress within therapy. Table 2 summarises these four factors and outlines the amount of influence upon therapy that is attributed to them (an educated guess that is often referred to as 'Lambert's pie').

As is evident from these estimates, the most influential factors are outside of the control of the therapist (extra-therapeutic) and only 15 per cent of therapeutic change is attributed to the specific characteristics of the model of therapy (techniques). Significantly the

Table 2 Four factors that affect therapeutic progress

Factor	Brief description	Impact
Extra-therapeutic	Specific client characteristics, outside events, etc.	40%
Relationship	Variables found across therapies	30%
Expectancy	Placebo, belief in treatment, etc.	15%
Techniques	Specific characteristics of the model of therapy	15%

Source: Based upon Asay and Lambert, 2000, and Lambert and Barley, 2002.

major factor that is at least partially within the control of the therapist is the relationship between counsellor and client. Although 30 per cent still appears to be a relatively modest factor of change, the work of Lambert and colleagues would suggest this to be the major facet that therapists have some influence upon.

At this stage we can breathe a sigh of relief, as in general the research evidence does support the work that we undertake. The confusing element is therefore assessing which model of therapy works best. Despite there being a convincing body of literature noting the equivalent effectiveness of approaches, it is impossible to ignore that this is not the view held by numerous policy-makers. Thus, concurrent to the research that has been accruing (some of which is noted above), institutions such as the NHS in the UK have developed with a very different outlook of the evidence (see Sackett, 1996, for an overview of the commonly used levels of evidence). The adoption of a very stringent, monodimensional view of research means that a lot of good-quality evidence is sidelined and ignored when drawing up models of good practice. With the fear of losing the trainee focus of the book we stop here with this issue and return to it in Chapter 4. At this point we reflect upon an activity in which we encourage you to consider how you might evaluate your therapeutic practice and reflect upon what evidence you think is important when judging your work in this way.

ACTIVITY 4: Are we all dodos?

If we can accept that all therapies can be beneficial in some circumstances, then what is it that supports psychological change in people? If there are active ingredients to what we offer, what could they be? This activity moves away from considering broad therapeutic approaches and gets individuals considering their own personal therapeutic practice. In particular, we hope that readers contemplate how they conceptualise the work that they do. Whilst doing so, in much the same way as Activity 3, we also encourage reflection upon how others may perceive their 'evidence'. The title of the exercise refers back to the dodo bird verdict noted in the previous section and sets the scene for questioning whether there are common factors between all therapies.

This activity attempts to:

1   get readers to reflect upon their conceptualisation of successful therapy
2   encourage individuals to consider what the active ingredients of successful therapy are in their work

and

3   encourage readers to consider how the general public or the broader profession would receive the way one assesses successful therapy.

The activity

For this activity we would like you to create a journal entry. We choose a journal entry as we hope that this will enable you to ponder things relatively freely – most people keep a pretty close eye on reflexive journals and do not just let anyone read them. The task is to reflect upon the four questions noted in Activity Box 4. At first glance these seem relatively straightforward, but often they are actually quite difficult to pin down.

ACTIVITY BOX 4

Are we all dodos?

Write a journal entry reflecting on the following questions:

- Are you any good as a counsellor?
- What do you perceive as the *active ingredients* within your work?
- What evidence from your practice would you use to support your claim?
- How would outsiders view your answers?

Following on from this discussion we would encourage you to reflect upon your answers in light of those we provide from our students. Additionally, we would also encourage you to talk further to peers, colleagues or even within your own therapy about such issues.

Your findings

Now let us guess: you thought you were OK as a counsellor? In fact, you probably thought you were above average. This would be no surprise as research does indicate that most counsellors put themselves in this category. The unfortunate side of things is that we can't all be above average. That would be impossible! So, if we probe a little deeper, what do you perceive to be the active ingredients in what you offer? Was it the purity of the psychological theory that you adopt? Or something more general like the quality of the relationship that develops? It may be something altogether different, like the colour of your wallpaper – who knows?

The second half of this exercise attempts to get you to add some substance to your thoughts. What do the active ingredients within your work actually manifest as? It is likely that some of this will be difficult to put into words, but we would encourage you to try. Once you have something it's then time to consider what others might think of your answer. As this is an activity to do on your own, be honest and don't hold back. Do you really think that others would go with your answers? Maybe they would find them woolly, too soulless or just downright ridiculous. Furthermore, they might not be firmly embedded in a particular school of psychological thought. Where do you fit into the bigger picture?

Our findings

Within our teaching it is common to get people to reflect upon this question in a counselling-skills activity. Specifically, we would provide a substantial period for individuals to practise listening skills whilst the person talking reflected upon their practice. Such space allows for some soul searching about the meaning of therapy (to them) and generally provides lots of thought-provoking feedback about the notion of evidence.

To begin with we will briefly reflect upon whether our trainees think they are any good. The answer they generally give when considering the question … well understandably they think they are OK, probably giving themselves a four on a scale of one to five (one being very poor and five being excellent). This commonly moves discussions on to reflect that this may not be a static score. Some days they would rate themselves a five or, on bad days, a one or a two. Such a variation raises the issue of what constitutes good and bad days. What are the active ingredients to therapy in their eyes? As with the components of Michael Lambert's pie (discussed earlier in this chapter) common issues can generally be summarised as the techniques utilised and the relationship fostered. No surprises there then.

Let's now move to consider how individuals come to the conclusion that they are good therapists. Initially we have to examine the gut, or more specifically the gut reaction. This is a phrase that can hide a multitude of sins and yet it reoccurs time and time again in training sessions (Interviewer: 'Why did you do that with your client?', Counsellor: 'Well … I guess it was a gut reaction'). So, is what we have established here that counsellors and psychotherapists often attribute their behaviour in sessions to stirrings in their bellies? Well, we guess the answer is no (or hope this is not the case in a majority of instances). Instead we begin to scratch the surface of the richness of therapy. As much as we may desire a neat and tidy answer, this is not always possible. And, as much as we hope for a practice always to have a firm rationale, we are all aware of times when something just *felt* right. Such a process would however be difficult to explain to those outside of the therapeutic world.

Two final, more conservative, responses, are 1) the knowledge that trainees are working stringently to a psychological framework or 2) the answers from client reports (questionnaires or conversations). The former can provide secure home bases for practitioners and consequently a sound rationale for the decisions that are made (Counsellor: 'I adhere stringently to the person-centred theory and that's what is important for good practice'). The latter can provide compelling evidence straight from the horse's mouth (Counsellor: 'My clients always say they benefit from our meetings' or 'My CORE scores always display that clients benefit from our meetings'). These statements are rife with problems. However, unlike the problem with our guts noted above, it is generally felt that they do look good to outsiders!

Discussion

Unlike Activity 3, this activity purposefully gets individuals to reflect upon their own skills as a practitioner. As a consequence this can often be a little unsettling for some counsellors. For instance, encouraging trainees to reflect upon the quality of their practice may make some realise that they are not actually providing a very useful service. Alternatively, it may be that practitioners realise that they have no sense of what is beneficial in the work they undertake. For trainers, it is obviously not our hope to cause unease or distress (well most of the time anyhow), and sensitive issues may arise which can be processed within group work (e.g. normalising people's anxieties about responding to gut reactions) or on a one-to-one basis outside of the class. It is, however, not the job of counsellor trainers to shy away from important issues either, and questioning the impact of therapeutic work is incredibly important. Thus, despite the personal questions that may be raised when offering this activity, we feel that it has been a very valuable process in counselling training.

Now think to the future. You're going to a job interview and one of the interviewees asks you whether you can provide evidence that you are an effective counsellor. Last night, in a moment of inspired clarity, you collated five years of outcome-measures scores related to your practice. Here your scores clearly reflect that 80 per cent of the clients you have worked with during this time period have shown an improvement. The panel are impressed and they offer you the job. In another instance you answer the same question by reflecting upon the verbal feedback that clients make at the end of sessions. This time you don't get the job. This may be a far cry from reality but interest in measurable therapeutic outcomes is increasing. In our groups there is always a section of individuals who use outcome measures and a section that do not. Numbers, as we will discuss in Chapter 6, provide compelling headlines that feel comfortingly definite. Maybe, just maybe, those who are skilled in producing these headlines (individuals and organisations) will be advantaged in the future over those who are not.

A final reflection for this activity is that it need not solely be a training activity. In the spirit of reflexive practice this may actually be an activity that counselling supervisors intermittently introduce into their practice with supervisees, or that counsellors take to supervision. As practitioners we feel that it is important to continuously reflect upon our practice. Thus, spending some time reflecting upon how effective we view our own practice may prove incredibly useful and open up doors to personal and professional development.

The student voice: Nadim Siddiqui

I agree with the authors' statement that this chapter addresses what are probably the hottest and most fundamental topics in the world of counselling, i.e. 'Does therapy work?' and 'Which approach works best?' The chapter is therefore useful in bringing to students' attention that the question is not as straightforward as might first be thought. The authors' obvious answer is unambiguously stated (or admitted) – CBT is usually best. Thankfully we are invited to dig a little deeper: 'What do we mean by "CBT"?' and 'What do we mean by "best"?'

So, what is CBT then? Usually the CBT offered up in comparisons is traditional, mainstream, second-wave CBT, with little reference or consideration to the revolution taking place in third-wave mindfulness-based approaches. It is interesting that as other therapies are being asked to prove their worth (often against second-wave CBT), third-wave CBT has had to engage in exactly the same process to gain acceptance with mainstream CBT. Some of this work has challenged some of the most fundamental premises of second-wave CBT, for example, 'Do we need to challenge thoughts in cognitive-behaviour therapy?' (e.g. Longmore and Worrell, 2007).

What works best? From Thought Box 2 and Activity 3, my firm belief was that CBT is undoubtedly the best therapy for most problems. As well as being a counselling psychology student, I am qualified in both CBT and the person-centred approach. The pro-CBT evidence I cited when completing these activities was the widespread and convenient view that NICE take of CBT. I also argued:

> Would you prefer to accept a medical or surgical treatment that had been subjected to Randomised Control Trials (an approach to research that examines interventions in a way that attempts to control as many variables as possible), or one mainly supported by qualitative case study material? If the answer is that you prefer the RCT-backed treatments for medical or surgical interventions, then why would you opt for a psychological approach mainly supported by (potentially) less vigorous tests?

The weakness in my argument is the apparently strong evidence from the common factors camp, armed with and fed by Lambert's pie (e.g. Asay and Lambert, 2000). Lambert makes an educated guess that the active ingredients of therapy are: 40 per cent what happens outside therapy, 30 per cent the client–therapist relationship, 15 per cent the therapeutic techniques used and 15 per cent the expectations the client has of the therapy – not great news for the technique- and procedure-driven, manualised world of CBT.

The Lambert's-pie deliberation is simply not the case from my own therapeutic experience, and I struggle to accept this apparent 'reality'. Other students in this exercise cited Mick Cooper's *Essential Research Findings in Counselling and Psychotherapy: The Facts are Friendly* (2008), which from my reading was not at all warmly disposed to CBT. One of the main anti-CBT arguments cited here is allegiance effects; i.e. that most of the pro-CBT research is flawed by people carrying out the research having vested interests in the CBT model. Apparently, pro-dodo-bird proponents do not appear to receive similar critiques and, therefore, in my view, do not seem to be guilty of the same crime. Back to the exercise: frankly, as a CBT-based trainee, I felt as if I was under assault. Whilst this was uncomfortable, it is an absolutely essential questioning and self-questioning process that is at the heart of the reflective and scientist practitioner frameworks that underlie counselling and psychotherapy.

Reflecting upon the above challenge to CBT led me to undertake further investigations. For instance, the dodo bird verdict relies on meta-analysis (the amalgamation of several studies). However, meta-analysis can take the dross of individually negative studies to produce the gold of a positive pooled result (Feinstein, 1995). Meta-analyses may therefore resemble alchemy. Further, Ghaemi (2009), in a statistical review of meta-analyses, concluded that the less heterogeneous the studies, the more valid the meta-analysis. In other words in reaching the dodo bird verdict Luborsky, Singer and Luborsky (1975), and their latter-day disciples, are comparing apples with oranges. So what are the differences between these apples and oranges? The apples are that NICE focused on chronic cases with very specifically identified and diagnosed problems. Most of the non-CBT research (the oranges) looked at in reaching the dodo bird verdict appear to be in primary care-type settings with clients seen early on in the presentation of their difficulty, where natural, spontaneous recovery is more common (Clark, Fairburn and Wessely, 2008). Perhaps another way of putting it is that the dodo bird verdict is a bit like looking at a variety of plants with a large magnifying glass. The trouble is that the magnifying glass is blurred, unfocused and scratched; you look at a wide variety of plants and reach the conclusion that 'Oh look, they're all green!' Well that's true, but it does not inform us of very much.

For me the activities in this chapter ticked numerous boxes for individuals learning about therapeutic research. These included promoting self-awareness, encouraging practice-based learning, looking at knowledge in action, the integration of theory and practice, problem setting and problem solving, and the element of surprise/improvisation and reflection in action (Schön, 1987; Strawbridge and Woolfe, 2010). Arguing the case for an approach that you are not embedded in, as well as exercising critical thinking skills, can also be highly instructive in consolidating your own theoretical and practice base.

The main learning experiences I gained from the exercises and chapter were:

- Don't accept that an opinion is correct just because a big name has argued it. Question it with all the critical thinking skills you have at your disposal.
- Critical thinking should be applied to other approaches and also to your own. Be suspicious of religious zeal: 'That's not person centred', or 'That's not CBT!'
- Be open to other potential ways of working by being pluralistic, integrative and eclectic; therapeutic practice can go beyond being entrenched in one or two approaches in which you have been trained.
- In contrast to the above point, having a home base is comfortable. Making for a solid island in stormy weather helps stop you being washed away. The concept of core competencies could help guide you.

- Just because there is work that argues against your home base position, don't conveniently ignore it. It's not honest or scientific.
- If you don't have the confidence and material to argue your case, no one else will do it for you. The exercises are a wake-up call to get equipped to stand your ground and defend your position, from an acceptant perspective.

The chapter and exercises rammed home for me that we are all in the same business really – we are all endeavouring to be professional therapists, who need to be open and honourable in what we apply and what evidence we choose to cite. Sometimes we can be guided by ancient wisdom:

> Exercising the right of occasional suppression and slight modification, it is truly absurd to see how plastic a limited number of observations become, in the hands of men with preconceived ideas. (Galton, 1863: 267)

Summary points

- Evaluating whether therapy works and which therapeutic approach is best is an incredibly complex business.
- Counsellors are well versed in the arguments against counselling.
- Counsellors are not always well informed about the research that supports their practice.
- There is a rich history of research into therapeutic approaches. Understanding this history may support counsellors in providing a rationale for the work that they undertake.

FURTHER READING

Mick Cooper's text *Essential Research Findings in Counselling and Psychotherapy* would be a great next step for the content of this chapter. This book is presented with counsellors and psychotherapists in mind and, in our view, provides an impressive summary of the literature related to this territory.

Cooper, M. (2008) *Essential Research Findings in Counselling and Psychotherapy: The Facts are Friendly*. London: Sage.

For those with the inclination to dig a little deeper, two fantastic texts in this area are:
Duncan, B., Miller, S., Wampold, B. and Hubble, M. (2010) *Heart and Soul of Change: Delivering What Works in Therapy*, Second Edition. Washington: APA.
Norcross, J. (ed.) (2011) *Psychotherapy Relationships that Work: Evidence-based Responsiveness*, Second Edition. Oxford: Oxford University Press.

We must also not forget the guidelines that are produced by organisations such as NICE in the UK. These provide very influential summaries of research findings using a systematic review process. See, for instance, www.nice.org.uk.

3

What is Research?

Abstract

This chapter takes a step backwards from Chapter 2 and examines what research actually is. The term itself is one that some individuals warm to easily, whilst it instils fear in others. In this chapter we therefore unpack some of the ways in which research is viewed and highlight that all counsellors and psychotherapists are engaged in activities that could easily be reframed as research. As we move through the chapter we outline a number of thought-provoking activities that purposefully help the reader to identify their existing experience and skills relevant to undertaking such work. Fingers crossed, research may not be so daunting after all. In checking out the content of the chapter, we then hear from Laura Cutts, a trainee counselling psychologist, about her perceptions of what has been written. To end, we highlight some useful texts for readers with a thirst for more information about where research and therapy cross over.

THOUGHT BOX 3

What does the word 'research' conjure up for you?

Consider:

- Who conducts research? And what do they look like?
- What is a research activity?
- How much does research influence your practice?

Find the fear (of research) and do it anyway

When considering the first question posed in Thought Box 3, what came up? Often the image of beardy men in white coats wielding clipboards crops up somewhere.

Additionally, in thinking about what constitutes research activities, did you think of statistical tests, complex mathematical formulae, strange language and complex terminology? If this is so, you are not alone; these are the attitudes and behaviours that we need to work with if we are to demystify research and bridge the divide between practice and research. This chapter hopes to provide a realistic sense of what research actually is. We do not want to shy away from the fact that some research does comply with the aforementioned criteria; however, this is far from the norm in present-day counselling and psychotherapy research. In years gone by, behaviourist psychologists such as Watson, Skinner and Pavlov did work in a way that complies to the stereotype above. They ran experiments using dogs, rats, pigeons and, in cases such as that of little Albert (Watson and Rayner, 1920), babies! Time has, however, moved on, and although there are psychologists who still work with animals, most of the work that is of use to therapists utilises human participants. Furthermore, as people have become more sensitive to ethical considerations within research with human participants (see Chapter 8 for more on this), it would be mightily unusual to obtain ethical clearance to condition a child to be frightened of furry animals and Father Christmas's beard nowadays (once again see the case of little Albert noted above – the latter example did actually happen).

The third question to consider in Thought Box 3 was 'How much does research influence your practice?' This seems incredibly important! After all, what use is any research if no one uses it? If you belong to a professional counselling or psychotherapy organisation, what happens to the research journal in your household? Does it hit your doormat only for the neat Cellophane wrapper to remain unopened? Or, if it does get opened, are the titles of the papers impossible to understand and seemingly have little or no relevance to your practice? If any of these examples reflect your behaviour/experience it might be comforting to know that you are not alone. Sadly, from our perspective, these sentiments are not unusual, and research even supports the notion that practitioners do not view research to be of great importance to their practice (e.g. Morrow-Bradley and Elliott, 1986; Orlinsky et al., 2001).

In accounting for the lukewarm reception that research often receives from counsellors and psychotherapists in the UK, we need to consider why this may be. After all, if we look at the historical roots to all of the major therapeutic paradigms (psychodynamic, cognitive-behavioural and humanistic), research has underpinned the development of each theory. Sigmund Freud viewed himself as a scientist, admired Charles Darwin and pioneered case-study work in psychotherapy (e.g. Freud, 1901/1990). At the roots of CBT, individuals such as Aaron Beck and Albert Ellis were not afraid of developing questionnaires and using experimental research designs (e.g. Beck et al., 1961; also see Chapter 6 for more on this type of research). Finally, let's not forget that the most eminent of humanistic psychologists and creator of the person-centred approach to therapy, Carl Rogers, was at the fore of the qualitative research movement (Rogers, 1985; also see Chapter 7 for more about this type of research). Thus, research is firmly at the base of all major therapeutic approaches and yet, somewhere along the line, practice and research appear to have been separated.

Let's reflect upon the development of counselling in the UK at this point. Commonly the beginnings of the counselling movement are noted to have been established in the early to mid-twentieth century. Organisations such as the Marriage Guidance Council (now Relate) were created and during the 1960s the first university counselling service was set up at Keele University. Another key moment was the creation of the British Association for Counselling (now the British Association for Counselling and Psychotherapy [BACP]) in 1977. This process of evolution occurred somewhat differently to practices in other countries and the emphasis on developing therapeutic skills has commonly taken priority over research awareness. As the sands shift towards creating a more research-informed practitioner base, organisations such as the BACP and the British Psychological Society (BPS) now emphasise the importance of research. In the former's case, this can be seen very clearly in the introduction of research skills into the core curriculum of accredited courses and the publication of self-commissioned research texts such as Mick Cooper's *Essential Research Findings in Counselling and Psychotherapy: The Facts are Friendly* (Cooper, 2008) and John McLeod's *Case Study Research in Counselling and Psychotherapy* (McLeod, 2010). In the case of the BPS, it is notable that counselling psychology programmes have all developed into Doctoral-level awards. The sands have most definitely shifted and we hope that this text contributes to the development of a more research-informed practitioner base in at least a small way.

You may have noticed that we have yet to answer the question 'What is research?' Instead we have reflected upon the potential fear that surrounds research, and highlighted how practice and research have become distanced from one another in the UK. Rest assured, we are getting there, but we ask you to bear with us a little longer. Before we get to a definition we want you to consider *your* existing knowledge of research and to reflect upon how our students commonly perceive research in the first week of their training.

ACTIVITY 5: What do YOU bring to the world of research?

Often the first training session on a research methods module is a daunting place. Research issues might have been played around with in other parts of the standard training programme, but it is often the research methods unit where things start to get serious. It is at this point that the word 'research' generates a big 'R', and becomes 'Research' – if not 'RESEARCH!!!' – as thoughts turn to the dissertation. Some individuals may find themselves in a research methods module purely because they need to be there for accreditation purposes (rather than for its own intrinsic worth) or a professional and personal development opportunity. Others might already be straining at the leash to get on with unpacking their burning research question and writing the dissertation. It may be a daunting place too for the trainer who perhaps is rather more attuned him- or herself to practice. Whatever the flavour of the group, there is likely to be a pool of emotions around which to provide a fertile place to start discussions.

This activity attempts to:

1 harness some of the energy that surrounds the introduction of research into the counselling and psychotherapy world
2 support individuals in finding out that they are not as novice-like to research issues as they may think

and

3 enable the reader to identify an area of research interest.

The activity

We often begin a research module with a full community meeting in which individuals can share their thoughts and feelings about the research process with a wide selection of others. In the case of a book like this, such a resource is not on hand, and so we ask readers to stop and reflect upon a number of questions before moving on to the next section. We therefore ask you to spend approximately 15 minutes pondering the questions outlined in Activity Box 5. We don't like to be prescriptive but you may find it useful to write down your answers in a research journal for future reference. It's always interesting to see how research interests unfold, and it's often difficult to retrace your footsteps accurately at later stages. You never know, if you are completing a dissertation this may become very useful fodder at some point in time.

ACTIVITY BOX 5

What do YOU bring to the world of research?

Please answer the following questions:

- Who are you? And why are you reading about research?
- What is your experience of research?
- What are your specific research interests?

Your findings

Once you have noted down answers to the three questions that we have asked, it is important to reflect upon the answers you have come up with. Examine them in some detail and consider what you think and feel about their content. Below we raise some questions that will help you to consider your answers before introducing common answers from our trainees in the next section.

To begin with it would be interesting to notice the excitement or reticence that you have towards the subject matter – how does who you are fit with why you are reading this text? Maybe you are one of the people noted above who is having to do a module on a course because it's a compulsory unit, or maybe you are one of the people who is excited by the potential of investigating something in depth. Alternatively you may fall somewhere in the middle, or have noted down something completely different. One of the joys of any open question is that you are never entirely sure of the answers people may come up with.

Next we come to the experience of research that you already have. Within the groups that we run it is usual for students to gain insights into the wealth of experience that they already have to develop upon. Fingers crossed, you will notice something similar in your answers. It is not unusual for people to have taken part in interviews or completed questionnaires prior to beginning taught research input. Increasingly therapists have even taken part in research studies focusing on elements of their practice. All of this provides useful foundations for studies in this area.

One thing that won't be apparent on working on your own is the breadth of research interests that therapists often have. Therapy is such a massive entity that the territory in which research interest falls can be very varied. For some, there is a clear area of interest from the outset (e.g. I'm (TH) interested in therapeutic work with young people and William is captivated by spiritual issues in therapy) whilst others have to undertake a little bit of searching. To provide some yardsticks to other individuals' experiences it seems appropriate to move on to reflect upon the different types of answers that we receive to the same questions in our student groups.

Our findings

Once trainees in our classes have completed the same task that you have just undertaken (usually in pairs) we ask for two types of feedback. First we ask for general feedback in the full student group about the first two questions before asking everyone to share their area of research interest. In this section, we briefly summarise the typical answers that arise during this process. It would be useful for readers to reflect upon their own answer to the questions in relation to this feedback.

Who are you and what do you think and feel about undertaking a research project?

(This question is slightly different to the one we asked you – this accounts for the different context in which it is asked.)

Commonly the first part of this question is a relatively simple task to complete: however, some counsellors and psychotherapists may not view it as straightforward – in essence we hope to elicit student names rather than existential discussions. The second element usually varies from person to person. There are always individuals who are anxious and daunted about undertaking a piece of research ('I'm not sure if I can do it'), those who resent the fact they are on the module ('I applied to do a counselling course, not a research course') and those who are excited by the prospect of undertaking a piece of research ('I can't wait to get my teeth into it').

What is your experience of research?

The first question then feeds into the answer to this one. Often anxieties are fuelled by limited knowledge or misconceptions about research. Initially there is a feeling of ignorance and naivety within the group; however, when pushed a little further it is evident that most of the group have been involved in research activities before. Group members share experiences of taking part in the research projects of others (e.g. interviews with other counselling researchers or focus groups about how much they like something like Marmite), using research tools in their practice (e.g. self-devised questionnaires to record general information or standardised questionnaires such as the CORE-OM) and undertaking research activities in previous work/studies (e.g. collating organisation audit data or working as a researcher at a university). Although it is not always openly acknowledged, all of the groups we work with have a wealth of research experience.

What are your specific research interests?

This is a difficult question to summarise in such a short space. Individuals' interests vary massively but there is always a direct point of connection with trainees. For instance, there is often a link to personal practice, whether this is the inner working of their client work, the particular setting in which they work, or the therapeutic approach they work from. For others, there may be a very personal connection to their lives such as bereavement, spirituality or substance misuse. Finally, there are always a number of people who solely have an academic interest in a particular topic. Needless to say, such varied motivations lead to a very broad array of research interests. (For information, we continue reflecting upon individuals' areas of interest in the next chapter of this book.)

Discussion

Commonly counsellors and psychotherapists feel inexperienced in research and reticent towards undertaking a research project. Although there are those who take to it like a duck to water, this is often overshadowed by the majority who feel apprehensive. Despite this, when reflecting upon individuals' experiences, it is often evident that people are actually quite well versed in research activities. They just didn't know it. This experience includes theoretical understanding and experience of collecting information (e.g. making notes) and making sense of it (e.g. summarising the issues that clients present with). This process of unpacking people's research experiences therefore helps to challenge explicitly the notion that the group are inexperienced. It also highlights that the task for counsellors is more a case of harnessing their knowledge rather than learning it afresh.

In identifying research interests early on we are able to develop a network of students with similar topics. The building of a research community is important as often research can be seen as a lonely endeavour. Given the reservations that practitioners may already have about such pursuits, developing some method for peer support can prove very useful. Further, counselling by its very nature is an insular activity that exists in the confines of necessary confidentiality. The training course and supervision are therefore two of the very few arenas where counsellors and psychotherapists can talk about their practice. A research forum, or some type of counselling research group, can act as a method of enhancing dialogue and support. This will be considered further in Chapter 9 of this book.

What is research?

In reflecting upon the above activity, the breadth of research interests that emerge provides an indication of the areas that therapists may consider researching. Such a list also gives an insight into what research is and how, in reality, everything is fair game for being researched. It is, however, notable that in a profession that often prizes philosophical and theoretical musings it still remains difficult for research to have a significant impact. Furthermore, as mentioned earlier, practitioners often view research as something that other people do and of little relevance to their own actual practice (Morrow-Bradley and Elliott, 1986). Is there any way beyond such sentiments?

Without a doubt, the world of research is beginning to have a huge impact upon our everyday work. It is increasingly common for service providers to be asked for evidence supporting what they do before getting money out of funding bodies, and to provide evidence of continuing their good work once they have it. All too often, such a process of monitoring and evaluating counselling and psychotherapy services is of a poor quality or completely absent. We therefore enter into the harsh Darwinian therapeutic waters in which only the fittest will survive. But this leads to the question, the fittest at what? Do the methods that are commonly advocated truly display a better end product? Or, do they just reflect that they are better at completing certain questionnaires? Here you may reflect upon the answer you gave to Thought Box 2 in Chapter 2 – 'Which approach to therapy works best?' – and contemplate how your therapeutic approach of choice is doing in the tree of life.

At this point, it is time to stop stalling and answer the question posed in the title of this chapter: 'What is research?' Our starting place is that research can be understood to be:

> ... original investigation undertaken in order to gain knowledge and understanding. (Research Assessment Exercise, 2005: 34)

This definition comes from the process that has been utilised to evaluate higher education institutions and ultimately to create league tables about their standing in this field (the Research Assessment Exercise, or RAE – now the Research Excellence Framework, or REF). It is therefore quite a common conceptualisation of research and, although it does continue to provide a little more clarity, it is striking how broad we can define research. A question you might want to ponder is, 'Does this definition reflect what you do in your therapeutic practice?' – more bluntly, 'Are counselling and psychotherapy relationships research activities?' Needless to say some readers will agree with this sentiment and some readers won't, but the idea that therapy is a research endeavour is a very interesting one.

Probably a more useful way of formulating research is by breaking it down into its key stages. Research is often cast as the bad guy and can be stereotyped by the completion of lots of questionnaires that you then need to be an amazing statistician to make sense of. However, although we acknowledge the importance of such work, we would like to reiterate once again that this is by no means the definitive type of research. John McLeod (a name that you will notice crops up throughout this text) describes research as needing to contain the following:

1 Critical enquiry – it is a human tendency or need to learn, to know or solve problems.
2 Process of enquiry – it a series of steps or stages.
3 It is systematic.
4 It produces propositions or statements.
5 The findings are judged according to validity, truthfulness or authenticity.
6 It is communicated to interested others.
(Summarised from McLeod, 2003: 4)

Once again, such a definition proves incredibly open; however, identifying these core elements helps to reflect the values that researchers hold onto tightly. This is not to say that poor or useless research isn't conducted. Often people get led down stuffy pathways, spend thousands of pounds and only end up finding something that we already knew. Some may even argue that some industries do this as a form of unscrupulous advertisement, but we will leave such discussions to the investigative reporters such as Ben Goldacre for the time being – see the text *Bad Science* (2008) for more on this. So, instead of getting led down this less desirable path, we would emphasise the exciting explorative dimensions to research that in many ways echo processes in good therapy. As Einstein once said, 'If we knew what it was we were doing, it would not be called research, would it?'

If we return to the overview of the research process provided by John McLeod, there are a few areas to unpack further – these are done so in more depth in his book *Doing Counselling Research* (McLeod, 2003), but we provide a short overview here. First, it is useful to note that research is a critical enquiry in which the researcher wishes to find out something more about a particular phenomenon (e.g. 'Am I any good as a therapist?' or 'What may be a useful way of engaging with clients online?'). This is nothing out of the ordinary and we are likely to undertake such tasks every day on a small scale. The next two points begin to suggest that the activity is more than your everyday musing over what type of cheese to buy in the supermarket. Here it is necessary that the research process follows a series of well-thought-out steps (in the case of cheese maybe I need to factor into my decision-making cost what I'm planning on eating it with, air miles, animal welfare or even allergies). The process should be transparent, appropriately rigorous and be able to withstand challenge. If it does not meet these criteria then the validity of any findings may be questioned, as noted in point five of McLeod's list – 'The findings are judged according to validity, truthfulness or authenticity'. Furthermore, in conducting a piece of research, there should be practical implications and recommendations for interested readers: Does it help us to improve practice? Or understand client difficulties better? and so on. A piece of research may be great, but if findings are not synthesised into a palatable format then they are not much use to anyone. The final point raised is often the point that our students omit – 'It is communicated to interested others'. Anxieties about the work, usually linked to questions about its quality and the researcher's competence, often get the better of people. This leads to much interesting and important research sitting on the shelves of research supervisors and gathering dust. The message here is: if you do something that's useful to you, have the conviction that it may also be useful to others and tell someone. We will talk about different avenues of disseminating research in Chapter 9.

So in thinking beyond the stereotyped outcome study, where else can research take us as counsellors and psychotherapists? One way of understanding the different types of research that people conduct divides studies into three major categories. These are:

1 *Input variables:* refers to the traits of the individuals involved (client and counsellor demo-graphics, attitudes, etc.) and the setting in which they meet.
2 *Process studies:* relates to the internal workings of the counselling session.
3 *Outcome studies:* pertains to the changes that occur directly or indirectly as a result of the counselling sessions.
(Based upon Hill and Williams, 2000)

Thus, although the latter category may get the most attention, the initial two are of great importance. For instance, it is important for individuals to reflect upon the settings in which we work, to devise models of good practice (an input variable). In addition, examining the inner working of the counselling relationship can provide important insights into the helpful aspects of change in psychotherapy (a process variable). Such work is essential for understanding therapeutic research and should complement outcome studies. After all, we may know that a certain approach works, but do we truly know what was the main factor that created change? One type of research is therefore very likely to raise questions related to the others.

Here we come to another activity that once again attempts to dispel some of the myths that may surround the world of research.

ACTIVITY 6: What might a research project look like?

As we have discussed above, the term 'research' can raise numerous anxieties. It gets banded around like a magic pill and increasingly the term 'research states …' has a currency within today's press. It is something to be held aloft and wielded with confidence. Something grand, something BIG! However, the reality is that research is often a much more modest endeavour. It follows logical rules and patterns and, although it scratches at the surface of the phenomenon under scrutiny, it raises more questions than answers. Considering this further, it's also noteworthy that the methods employed to collect information are often relatively simple – grand plans (without appropriate funding) often make poor research projects.

This activity attempts to:

1 help individuals to identify the common components of research projects
2 inform individuals of any gaps in the research process that may be evident

and

3 once again support the reader in finding out that they actually know more than they think they do.

The activity

This activity aims to dispel some of the myths that surround the world of research. In particular we intend to unpack the processes that take place in standard research projects. We would recommend you spend a little while reflecting upon these questions alongside research journals/articles that you may have to hand. If you don't have any, don't worry, note down anything that comes into your head based upon your own experiences or previous reading.

ACTIVITY BOX 6

What might a research project look like?

Consider:

- What major stages to a research project might there be?
- What might occur in the different stages identified?
- Do publications that you have read give an insight into the processes that research-ers undertake?

Your findings

So, what did you come up with? Let's take the first question – 'What major stages to a research project might there be?' It may be that this is a difficult question to answer. You may have little or no experience of research. In which case, you may talk, just as we do about counselling relationships, about research having a beginning, middle and end. Alternatively, you may have a very good grasp of the various procedures involved in conducting a research project. In this case, you may have fleshed out the skeleton quite considerably. In fact, you may have begun to identify different aspects of each stage that crop up through the lifespan of a research project. In doing so, you have taken us onto the second question posed.

In relation to the second question, there is a likelihood that you will have some sense of what a research project may look like. In particular you may have an idea that it could consist of using questionnaires, conducting interviews or hosting a focus group.

You may also have a sense of the need to examine the ethics of the work and the fact that some research gets published in journals. Maybe at this point you could rate your knowledge of the research process out of 10 (1 = knowing very little and 10 = being well informed). You may then want to do this again once you have read through the 'Our Findings' section for this activity below to see if your awareness has changed (you may want to do this at various intervals throughout the text).

Finally, reflect upon how you came up with the answers you arrived at for the activity. If you fleshed out the different stages, did you look at any research papers to see how others had gone about conducting the work? Often there are commonalities in the way that research is presented and this can provide an insight into the stages worked through. In fact, a good piece of research is often viewed as having a replicable design. So, the reporting should be transparent and clear to the reader.

Our findings

In synthesising the discussions that occur in our trainees' discussions, certain themes become very apparent. These are often chronological in order and ultimately it's notable that the groups are often successful in fleshing out the process together, thus creating a detailed overview of the process. Below are the common themes that often arise.

Planning research

This is identified as the initial phase of a research project. Commonly students are very aware that they have to complete a research proposal as an assignment. They are however less confident about what this may look like. There is a sketchy understanding of the need to conduct an initial review of the literature and to describe what it is you will be doing in the project, but at this stage not much more. The contents become a little clearer as we progress to the next phase.

Preparing for research

This stage could be viewed as a subsection of planning research, but here we have divided it up to reflect the more practical elements discussed. For instance, the groups are aware of the need to create information sheets and resources for the project. They are also mindful of the need for the project to be scrutinised ethically. Once all of these pieces are in place, discussions can include the need to set the research in motion. This may include having to arrange interviews or train individuals to use a certain questionnaire. It may also include reflecting upon particular contracts that are agreed with participants.

Doing research: data generation

For a group that often undermines their research awareness, this part of the research process generates much rich discussion. Trainees are often well versed in research methods that may be adopted. Methods such as interviewing, focus groups and questionnaires are always introduced. These are then unpacked to include sophisticated discussions such as the style of interview (structured or unstructured) or questionnaire (self-made or standardised). Additionally, critical discussion of the motivations for using such methods is often introduced (e.g. 'a questionnaire can reach more people quickly', or 'interviews enable the generation of rich data'). As things continue to emerge, some of the anxieties in the group begin to dissipate.

Data analysis

One area that does very little to alleviate anxieties is the area of data analysis. Trainees are often aware that this is something they will have to engage in, but less sure about what it actually entails. Occasionally individuals will be aware of specific techniques (e.g. grounded theory or t-tests – these are discussed briefly in later chapters), but often it is a new territory for most. However, having said that, it is clear that the skills of data analysis are rife in the room. Counsellors are often very good at recognising patterns and reflecting upon content. Likewise they regularly check out meaning with clients and use theory to guide practice. Such processes are essential when attempting to make sense of data.

Disseminating research

We include this section as an area that is very rarely offered by trainees. When floated as an idea, many do not see it as something they will do themselves. However, when discussing the many avenues of dissemination, most of the group acknowledge that they will be doing something in this area. This may be as small as a summary sheet of the research for those who took part; it may include conducting a training session with colleagues, or more adventurously publishing in a research journal. There are many other ways of getting research into the public domain and we would encourage people to consider how they may do so at early stages.

Discussion

At the outset of this activity there is often a sense that individuals know very little about the research process. As discussions progress, it becomes abundantly clear that this is far from the case. This is not to say that individuals can easily transfer their knowledge into practice, but it does help to demystify the research process. Specifically, it is reassuring to many that the skills they have as therapists stand them in good stead to undertake certain styles of research. For example, counsellors and psychotherapists are very well versed in ethics, contracting and questioning techniques and so on, and this should not be ignored.

In contrast to the knowledge that is often generated by large groups, clearly there are many gaps in the awareness of a number of individuals who undertake the activity outlined above. Much focus is placed upon the applied elements of data generation, and less upon the systematic processes involved in research design. Thus, the planning stages, and more specialised areas such as data analysis, are often covered in brief. Likewise dissemination of the findings generated within the work is often omitted altogether without a gentle prod from a group facilitator. In offering this activity we therefore hope that readers have been able to reflect upon the gaps in their own awareness of research. Hopefully, individuals may have also been aided by the comments noted above – to at least create a skeleton framework which they can consider developing as they read on.

The student voice: Laura Cutts

As a trainee counselling psychologist who is only too aware that the date of my research panel (where I have to present my planned research) is looming, this chapter definitely provided food for thought. I have attempted to present my reflections and response to the chapter in the paragraphs that follow, and hopefully these will serve to add to your initial thoughts following reading the material above. I focus initially on two of my responses to the material presented above, followed by a brief discussion of an additional point which potentially extends beyond the material already contained within the chapter.

When reading the questions in Activity Box 5 – 'What do YOU bring to the world of research?' – and reflecting upon the reported findings I was reminded of discussions with my peers on the Doctorate in Counselling Psychology. Looking back on the beginning of the course last year, even outside of the classroom I remember having conversations about people's research interests, how confident everyone felt in relation to conducting research, and the importance they placed on it. These conversations have continued and developed over the course of the year. What I have been fascinated to discover is that there is, as the chapter notes, such a massive variance in research interests. But on the whole, we all shared the same initial fears and concerns about the research element of our course. Even the most enthusiastic members of the group with regards to research had some worries, whether it was the scale of the project, knowing where to start, or settling on a specific research area. Nevertheless we have been able to see over the course of the year how our research ideas and plans begin at least to take shape. Activities and questions such as the ones posed in this chapter are a useful task to identify your worries and possible misconceptions. The heading 'Find the fear (of research) and do it anyway' seemed to sum it up for me! When reflecting on your worries and possible misconceptions in the way detailed in this chapter, you are able in some way to lessen the fear (hopefully!).

My second reflection focuses more directly on the topic addressed in the title of this chapter. Over the past year I have regularly asked myself the question posed here. This was initially prompted by an activity similar to the ones you have been asked to consider here, where as part of a focus group in university I was asked to consider what research really is. How do we define it? And I was stumped. I had considered the place of research in counselling and counselling psychology, and even asked myself the question: how commensurate are science and practice? But going back to the start and defining research seemed like a completely new challenge. According to my reflexive journal, I managed to get as far as 'a process of acquiring knowledge' and as a group we managed a few more statements of a similar generality. Following this exercise we were provided with the definitions included in this chapter, from the RAE and John McLeod, which did enlighten me further. The John McLeod definition in particular I think captures some of the additional points that escaped me when I was trying to answer the question. The idea that research is systematic is for me key in defining research: is this what distinguishes 'little-r research' from 'big-R Research'?

As a further reflection from reading this chapter I have been led to wonder: do we need to consider an additional question beyond the one posed in the title? Specifically –

What is good research?

As mentioned in the chapter, research has begun to have a large and important role in counselling. As a counselling psychology trainee I am asked to become a 'scientist-practitioner', where the world of science and research are somehow neatly interwoven with counselling practice (see Blair, 2010, for an introduction if you're interested). We were asked at the beginning of this chapter to consider the question 'How much does research influence your practice?' This is a topic that will be returned to within the following chapters, so I will not dwell on this now; however, for me it seems important first to consider *what* research?

As counsellors, therapists or counselling psychologists it seems perhaps that we need to know more than just what research is: we need to understand research, and know what good research, or evidence, looks like (Wheeler and Elliott, 2008). What constitutes good 'evidence'? It doesn't seem enough to read a research paper; if we are to be truly research-informed do we not need more than this? (See Stoltenberg et al., 2000: 630, for a discussion around the concept of 'informed consumerism'.)

Following the definition noted in the chapter above, McLeod notes that

> there are many ways of arriving at valid propositional knowledge in the field of counselling. (2003: 4)

He discusses the idea that 'research' equates to 'science', which I would guess may be at the root of many counsellors' fears about research discussed back at the beginning of this chapter.

But is *all* research equally valid? How, as trainees and qualified practitioners, do we discern and decide what makes a good research paper, and potentially therefore good evidence? There are mixed views on this complex issue and rather than attempting to go into the debate here, I will leave you with that additional question.

Summary points

- The term 'research' is viewed in a multitude of ways. Commonly it can be a source of much anxiety to counsellors, but it can also create much excitement.

- Counsellors and psychotherapists utilise research activities every day. They just don't call them research. They can be viewed as small-r research when contrasted to more formal activities which may be viewed as big-R Research.
- Research is difficult to define owing to the many different forms that it takes. It is often more useful to describe the different stages that individuals undertake in a project as this helps to demystify the process.
- Outcome research is just one strand of the research that counsellors and psychotherapists undertake. Research examining input variables and process variables can also be incredibly important.

FURTHER READING

There are now hundreds of texts that focus upon research. Some of these introduce the nature and purpose of research, whilst others are more applied and focus upon how to do research. Still, others combine these two goals. In addition to this, these texts include generic books such as John Creswell's excellent *Research Design: Qualitative, Quantitative and Mixed Methods Approaches* (2003), but also cover pretty much every professional discipline. In relation to the latter, counselling and psychotherapy is no different, and below we outline some of the more generic texts that you might find helpful in continuing your reading from this chapter.

Dallos, R. and Vetere, A. (2005) *Researching Psychotherapy and Counselling*. Maidenhead: Open University Press.
McLeod, J. (2003) *Doing Counselling Research,* Second Edition. London: Sage.
Sanders, P. and Wilkins, P. (2010) *First Steps in Practitioner Research: A Guide to Understanding and Doing Research in Counselling and Health and Social Care*. Ross-on-Wye: PCCS Books.
Timulak, L. (2008) *Research in Psychotherapy and Counselling*. London: Sage.

4

Preparing for Undertaking Research

Abstract

In this chapter we want to lead you gently into the whole area of undertaking research. In particular we focus upon several areas that we feel are essential for undertaking a successful research project. The first of these is the question that you come with. This could potentially be a vast territory within the world of counselling and psychotherapy research and is likely to need harnessing a little (or a lot). Following on from this, the need for critical thinking is discussed before moving on to consider the importance of passion within any long-term project. In combination, these latter two factors, we would argue, will help to see the creation of a successful research project. Following on from the discussion of these areas we then question the practicalities of undertaking a research project. Although the next chapter focuses more specifically on the challenges throughout the lifespan of a research project, here we question the fundamentals – for example, do you have enough space and money in your life to conduct a research project? We then consider the creative dimension of research before ending with a comment about the chapter from Pariya Habibi, a trainee counselling psychologist. A few key resources are then recommended to help you on your journey.

THOUGHT BOX 4

What is *your* burning research question?

Consider:

- What are you drawn to as a topic of intrigue? Maybe this is something about the setting of your practice, the internal working of your practice, or whether you are actually any good as a therapist.

Burning research questions

Let's begin by considering your answers to Thought Box 4 above: 'What is *your* burning research question?' Some of us have burning questions of a rather philosophical or somewhat abstract nature. For example, 'What is the relationship between therapy and spirituality?' or 'How do humanistic values manifest in therapy?' Others will be asking broad-ranged questions such as, 'Does (my) therapy work?' or 'Why do so few Black and Minority Ethnic men access therapy?' For many of us there are also niggling questions which arise from our own particular therapeutic practice. For instance, 'What are bereaved clients' experiences of therapy?', 'How do lawyers cope with secondary trauma?', or 'What are the therapeutic outcomes for my agency and how do they compare with results elsewhere?' These topics appear almost limitless and this is already reflected within the breadth of the literature in the therapeutic field.

Once a topic has been decided upon there needs to be a good fit between your research question and your chosen methodology. It is quite common for novice researchers to have, or to discover, a pet methodology that they want to apply to their research project. Certainly novice researchers (and indeed experienced researchers) are often drawn to either one or the other of quantitative or qualitative approaches (which we discuss further in Chapters 6 and 7). This is fine as long as this pet methodology does deliver (a) useful answer(s) to the research question. For example, if your research topic is 'What are bereaved clients' experiences of therapy?' then a survey of such clients will only deliver limited, if broad, data. In contrast, a group or series of individual interviews would hopefully yield richer data about the experience but from a smaller number of people. Immediately you can see the trade-offs involved – richness of data against breadth of data. Going back to the original research question, which focuses upon 'clients' experiences', it is probably safe to say that rich, deep data is what we are after. (A compromise position of mixed methods, say a survey plus some in-depth interviews, is a possibility but, be warned, it is often much more work.)

Having settled on which broad choice of qualitative, quantitative or mixed methods the question fits into, then more questions arise. For instance, 'Which measure do you use in quantitative research?' or 'Which methodology might you adopt in qualitative research?' At this point we wish to introduce two thoughts: one, 'What is an *elegant* choice?' (further discussed in West, 2011) and two, 'What *pragmatically* gets the job done?' Fortunately these are not mutually exclusive and often the most elegant choice of methodology is the one that gets the job done most easily and provides a good basis for writing and disseminating the finished research. Sometimes there will be two or more competing qualitative methodologies, or two competing quantitative measures that are fit for purpose. When confronted by such decisions we would encourage you to think critically and consider how each choice might pan out in the long run (possibly alongside a research supervisor).

The literature relating to therapy research is very frustrating. Most of it has been done in the USA, a lot of it with college students, and very little of it is qualitative. It is very easy for an open electronic search to yield a lot of such data that, if uncritically put together, would result in a lopsided literature review. It is important to notice the gaps that occur in the research literature and to ponder what this means. Gaps often mean that our research is breaking new ground, which is both exciting and frustrating at the same time. Exciting because your research should then generate quite a bit of interest when you have completed it, but frustrating in terms of how to do the literature review and how to discuss your findings. If there is a literature gap at the heart of your research, try some different terms in your electronic search, discuss it with your academic supervisor, look for 'grey' (unpublished) literature and above all tell your readers about it. If you really draw a blank, do not be despondent, as you're probably on to something. You will however have to think a little more laterally and search out relevant literature in neighbouring fields such as education, nursing and so on.

The importance of being earnest (or at least critical)

The above reflections begin to outline that decisions in research should not come without forethought. The practice of therapy, like any other human activity, can benefit from 'thinking outside of the box', and arguably a good research project could be based on encouraging a group of practitioners to do the same. Colin Feltham, one of our favourite writers on counselling, consistently invites us to consider critically such questions as, 'Do we need supervision forever?', 'Is training necessary?', 'Is statutory regulation a good and inevitable development?' and 'What's wrong with psychoanalytic therapy?' (Feltham, 2010). Even if exploring such fundamental questions does not provide an idea for a research project, the critical questioning and thinking behind these questions are worth taking into your work.

Many counsellors, when they first engage with research, want to ask basic questions about their own practice:

'What is the research evidence that underpins my practice?' (This can apply on both a macro level, reflecting upon the school of therapy that you adhere to, and on a micro level, looking at the particular intervention(s) used with your clients.)

'Does my practice actually benefit my clients?' And, if so, 'In what ways?'

'Who do I work best with and why?'

Many of these questions can also be applied both to the agency you work within and to counselling as a whole. When you look carefully at these questions it will soon become apparent that to answer them effectively would necessitate a huge (or several huge) research studies. For example, as we have discussed in 'The great psychotherapy debate' in Chapter 2, the question of which therapy is best for which client problems has been researched for well over 50 years, especially in the USA, and will continue to be so, not least because every new brand of therapy created has to 'prove' itself by setting up a research study in which it can demonstrate its effectiveness when matched against its more established rivals. Furthermore, to our mind, what works best on the micro level leads to research in which real-life therapy sessions are examined moment by moment (preferably on video). Such research, whilst of great importance, is very labour intensive.

By now you might be thinking: 'What is the point? I cannot possibly devote the time and resources necessary for such research.' True enough, you can't, but that does not mean you cannot design a more modest research project that can make a useful contribution to our understanding and practice of therapy. For example, the collection of routine client out-come data using standardised questionnaires (a process which has become commonplace in practice) does allow us to explore which clients are helped by which counsellors using which approaches. It would also be possible to target ex-clients from your agency who benefited especially well from counselling and explore what they think actually did help them best. Such studies can truly contribute to the greater body of knowledge. In being critical, however, it is always important to be mindful of their limitations and be transparent about them. The next activity considers some of the limitations within this book.

ACTIVITY 7: The importance of being critical

Being critical is an essential skill of a researcher. Here we invite you to adopt a critical stance to the contents of this book. We are very aware that individuals will perceive different strengths and weaknesses to the text and we now want to know what you think.
   This activity attempts to:

1   encourage individuals to think critically about the literature they are reading
2   help readers reflect upon the strengths and weaknesses of a piece of writing

and

3   provide material for the reader to reflect upon skills they wish to bring into their own work.

The activity

To get you thinking critically about a piece of writing, we offer ourselves up like lambs to the slaughter for you to do your best. If you are reading this text from front to back you will have already passed by Chapter 2, entitled 'The Research Underpinning Therapy'. Here we want you to revisit this (only briefly) with a view to reflecting in more depth on its content and style. In particular, we want to get you thinking about how transparent we have been about motivations in the chapter, how we have ultimately pulled it together, the foundations upon which we make claims, and the quality of the claims that we are making. Each of these issues is very important in writing academic work and we wonder what you think the strengths and weaknesses of this chapter are. (Do remember that being critical means considering both sides of the story and not just ripping it apart!) Activity Box 7 summarises this activity.

ACTIVITY BOX 7

The importance of being critical

Read Chapter 2 of this book with a view to considering its strengths and weaknesses. Consider the following questions:

- Are we, as the authors, transparent in our motivations within the writing? What might our biases (or stances) be?
- Is the writing style accessible? Is this a strength or weakness? Or, what sort of message does this convey?
- What source material is used to back up the claims we make? Is this of a good standard?
- Are our conclusions appropriately modest? Or are there unsubstantiated claims?

Your findings

First, we hope that the chapter gave you plenty of content to get your teeth into. Second, we hope that you heeded the suggestion to be balanced in your views! Or at least you saw some good bits somewhere. Now, our pride aside, what type of reflections did you make?

Did you get a good sense of who we are as authors and our motivations behind the work? Alternatively – were we hidden and purposefully leading, or misleading in our content?

In terms of the piece of writing, did you feel that it usefully combined academic rigour with accessibility? Or did it sway too far in one direction? Maybe we didn't reference enough, or referenced too much? Furthermore, maybe you thought the source material we used wasn't of a very high standard. These issues may lead into our final prompt question: were our assumptions appropriately modest?

Our findings

A good place to start here is with the Student Voice section within Chapter 2. Here Nadim has engaged in a useful way with the content we have presented. In particular, it's very helpful that Nadim has not been completely swayed with the argument that we have provided. He has responded by providing a thoughtful commentary that makes use of credible source material to present an alternative viewpoint. Such a response might make the beginnings of a fruitful academic debate, in which points and counterpoints could be considered and developed.

Within Nadim's response, it is useful to note how he questions the assertions behind the way evidence is manipulated in our writing. This links to the first question that we posed:

- Are we, as the authors, transparent in our motivations within the writing? What might our biases (or stances) be?

Here, the response does not challenge us directly but it does challenge the evidence that we use in creating our arguments, a factor which also links to our third and fourth questions:

- What source material is used to back up the claims we make? Is this of a good standard?
- Are our conclusions appropriately modest? Or are there unsubstantiated claims?

Thus, as with most arguments, if we pick at its foundations sufficiently, weaknesses will surface. Here, as a partial defence, we would possibly return to our second question to provide some context.

- Is the writing style accessible? Is this a strength or weakness? Or, what sort of message does this convey?

Understandably, Nadim does not mention the writing style of the chapter as it was not part of our request to him; however, as was indicated in the Introduction to this book, this text aims to be informed yet reader friendly. With this in mind, it is therefore likely that if we were producing a more academic text or piece of research, we would write in different ways. In doing so we might then be perceived as covering our bases more thoroughly.

Discussion

If we reflect upon our findings in relation to the literature the first point we would raise is the transparency behind our assertions. In our data source (Nadim's contribution), questions have been raised about the quality of the information we have utilised to construct our argument. Such a comment may indicate that our work is not appropriately reflexive or transparent, an important factor in the publishability of research (Elliott, Fischer and Rennie, 1999).

A second point that we would highlight is the need to be ready to question the foundations of any piece of academic writing, research or otherwise. Authors bring themselves to the table with their words and these inevitably inhabit particular world views. For instance, the hierarchy of evidence that NICE utilises to assess research might be situated within a reductionist medical-model frame that does not feel comfortable to therapists who often hold a more holistic view of the person. This is not to say that we should dismiss assessment frameworks completely, but we should become informed consumers of them, thus enabling us to become informed by research rather than directed by it (see Hanley et al., 2012). Such a dialogue is incredibly important and a fundamental part of the research process. Unfortunately, we observe all too often that this becomes more about battles between entrenched, immoveable positions rather than a process of learning.

All research goes through a critical peer review of sorts. This may involve being assessed by tutors or being reviewed by editorial boards of journals. This process can be unnecessarily brutal at times but it can also be incredibly fruitful and formative. Comments that are useful in nature can explicitly highlight that mistakes have been made, help to hone arguments and positively augment what has already been presented. We hope that you have found it helpful acting as reviewers for our work and see elements of the above in your critique.

Crimes of passion

Now that we have underpinned this chapter with the notion of critical thinking, we move on to consider a much less contained factor in research, passion. Consider the following quote from Aristotle:

> The law is reason, free from passion.

Such sentiments provide a view that passion can blinker one's thinking and thus the conclusions that are drawn may be less than helpful. We, however, feel that there is a fine line in research to straddle and that the risk is worth taking. At the outset of any research project, we would argue, there has to be a *passion* to know something more about a particular topic (even if this is to research a topic you don't care about, to learn about research methods). Quite a bit of the research process will be dull and boring, occasionally it will be very hard work, and it will likely take much longer than you originally planned. So starting with at least some passion for the topic can be helpful. Such passion should however not blind you from the obvious or lead you to be uncritical. It is important that researchers are reflexive about themselves and at least try to ask themselves some really awkward questions. It is also recommended that you keep a record of this process and write down your answers to these questions in your research diary. This may seem tedious but they may well prove very useful later. Your examiners, peer reviewers and your audiences at your presentations will undoubtedly ask some supportive and challenging questions of you!

Part of the challenge from that first moment of passion about a possible topic is designing a doable piece of research that does not lose the passion you have for the broader topic. Most research ideas, if carried out on the basis of the original passion, would take something like ten years to complete and would need a large research budget. This might well be worth doing, but not as your first piece of research! So, research has to be doable and has to yield some useful data if possible. This data may be about confirming something we already know, and that is fine. However, we should always be open to the possibility of being surprised, and sometimes these surprises come out of our apparent mistakes. (There is good pedigree here for important discoveries coming out of mistakes – it was certainly how the usefulness of penicillin was discovered!)

Passion is not enough. You need to be *motivated* too. You need to want to complete your research and not just take part in it. It helps if your research is for an academic qualification; or to strengthen the future of the agency you work for; or to help clients suffering with a particular problem; or some other reason or some combination of these. Research can be a lonely process and it helps if you have research *buddies* as well as a research supervisor. As with any sustained activity, doing research changes us. It has the potential to make us better practitioners, but it can cause tensions with colleagues who are not engaged in research. For instance, research can be associated with higher status than practice and this can cause friction. With this in mind, individuals should be cautious of the potential impact of their work on themselves and others.

John McLeod (2003), in discussing what research is, emphasises sharing the findings of our research to interested others. We owe it to ourselves and to our research participants to share what we have found. This can take a number of forms: seminars to colleagues; presentations at counselling and counselling research conferences; publication in a professional journal, book chapter or academic peer-reviewed journal; online publication on a website; or a combination of several of these (see Chapter 9 for more about issues of dissemination). We may actively choose to reach a number of different audiences. The worst thing is to do the research and then do nothing with it (see Chapter 8 about considering the ethics behind research). Getting back into the topic once you feel you've finished can be a major sticking point. Once again, passion can be a useful motivator.

Bias, stance and researcher 'objectivity'

It easy to see the researcher bias, or, as we prefer to refer to it, the 'researcher's stance', as a problem only for individuals using qualitative approaches. Surely quantitative researchers have eliminated or minimised bias in their carefully designed questionnaires and surveys, all carefully worded and piloted? Unfortunately this is not so simple an issue. Two of us have previously written:

> the researcher is at the very heart of decisions regarding the research process in this type of project as they predefine the terms they are measuring when operationalising variables and reducing them to measurable phenomena. The researcher is also able to predefine how the data can be handled. The power of the objective researcher to predefine hypotheses, variables and treatment of the data is surely a process that requires some reflection. A pretence at an unreal disinterest in the research and its outcome is a dangerous fallacy. It is far better to acknowledge what is at stake for the researcher. (Lennie and West, 2010: 86).

The researcher who has not carefully reflected on their research before gathering data might well be guilty of bias. The aware researcher knows what their stance is and takes steps to ensure the participants and the audience for their research study also know this (a mark of good-quality research noted in Chapter 7). Remember that research data has been collected at a point in time by that researcher with specific belief systems. Re-examining the research data ten years later might well give rise to a different analysis (e.g. new statistical tests for quantitative data or different cultural perceptions of qualitative data) and certainly the relevant literature will almost certainly have developed and moved on. One of us has carried out a study where different researchers from a variety of cultural backgrounds have analysed the same five interview transcripts with some interesting results (West, 2009).

Before we get swept away in our own passion for the subject matter, let's get a little more practical. Are you really in a position to undertake a project of this kind? The next activity aims to encourage individuals to reflect upon some of the issues that may get in the way.

ACTIVITY 8: The nuts and bolts of preparing to undertake a research project

We can romanticise about the nature of the research process as much as we like but we can't escape the practical realities of doing it. Research can be a very valiant endeavour in which we gain a greater insight into a little-known world. Behind this, however, is a lot of hard work and resources. This activity attempts to get people to consider how this might manifest within their lives.

This activity attempts to:

1   help the reader to consider the practical side of engaging in a piece of research
2   raise awareness to the issues that might get in the way of undertaking a research project

and

3   encourage the reader to reflect upon the support structures that they need in place to complete a piece of research.

The activity

This is a very brief activity that should only take a few minutes. Spend a short while reflecting upon issues that might stop you undertaking a research project. If you are already engaged in a piece of research you may want to consider what might lead to your having to leave it prematurely. Choose two of these and note them down on a piece of paper. Activity Box 8 summarises this activity.

ACTIVITY BOX 8

The nuts and bolts of preparing to undertake a research project

Jot down on a piece of paper two things that might get in the way of you undertaking a research project (or having to end it prematurely).

Your findings

What did you note down? Were these psychological, physical or practical issues? Alternatively, maybe you felt there was nothing stopping you. If this is the case, our findings may not be of much use. They may however highlight a blind spot, so we'd urge you to read on.

Our findings

Outlined below are some of the common themes that arise in our discussions with students.

Am I good enough?

This is probably the most common issue that we encounter with the trainees that we work with. Many of the issues below have been resolved (or not considered) by the time they arrive at our office. Therapists do not always follow traditional academic pathways and might be coming to a research programme numerous years after their first degrees (if they have one in the first place). Do however remember that you have been accepted onto the programme and there is some onus upon tutors in developing your skills too.

The concern of not being good enough is often linked to the critical nature of research activities too, with some people viewing the academic critique personally. Without a doubt this can be a difficult process and, if it is of any consolation, each of us still has similar doubts about the work that we present at times!

Can I afford the course?

Training courses are expensive. In fact research is expensive and people often underestimate its cost. The reason for this is that research is skilled work and needs an appropriate infrastructure to support it (e.g. library access, ethical committees, supervision, etc.). Furthermore, there is very little funding out there to support research training of counsellors and psychotherapists. People therefore often have to make a big financial decision about entering onto a programme.

Do I have the time?

Linked to the point above is the issue of time. Research can be difficult to fit into a busy life and the time spent working on it means that you can't be doing something else more financially rewarding.

Do I have a supportive infrastructure at home/work?

When considering the need for passion in research we must not forget those who have to suffer our dalliances with another time-consuming entity. This might be a spouse, partner, work colleague, friendship group or child. It will most likely impact upon them, and concessions often need to be made to make it workable in both directions. Do talk with others about how it might fit in. Those who take the main brunt of your distance will be those standing beside you in the graduation photographs, and their role should be heartily acknowledged.

Unforeseen life events or physical illness

This one always catches us by surprise. In almost every cohort of students we have worked with there are always individuals who have to take time away from their research projects due to unforeseen life events or illness. Most of the time this has been impossible to predict and where this is the case we would iterate that academic institutions are often as supportive and flexible as possible. Likewise, in the instance that illnesses are predicted or ongoing, plans can often be made with institutions to fit with your particular needs.

Discussion

Now we are not aware of literature related to the challenges people face whilst undertaking a therapy-based research project (apart from Ann Scott's (2008) interviews with Master's students discussed in Chapter 5). This therefore limits this discussion somewhat as we would hope to refer to this literature in an ideal world. Instead we will pick out a few headlines. In particular, we want to be realistic here. Although we do not wish to put anyone off doing a research project, the process isn't going to be for everyone. Going the distance is a real challenge and stepping into the ring can be a huge part of the process. Individuals may find hurdles in their way that prove insurmountable related to their academic skills, financial issues, personal lives or more generally their health, to name a few areas. We hope that in raising these issues you are able to consider what might get in the way for you. The next step, for those still wishing to continue, is to plan forward to prepare for such eventualities, an idea that we acknowledge is always easier to say than to do.

A final preparation point: creativity in research

Research is always a creative activity. You have to create a research design that leads to the creation of data. This data then leads to a creative synthesis of findings that needs to be presented in a form that you create. Thus, another element of the research process is to prepare for the need to be creative. Below we initially consider research that embraces creativity, with the hope of enticing back into the fray those whose senses may have been dulled by the nuts and bolts of research activity above. Following this, we briefly reflect upon some more generic creative processes within research. We then end with a poem.

> The researcher's and poet's responsibility, and talent, is not just to 'tell it like it is' but to add a deeper sounding. (Saunders, 2003: 185)

Hopefully your research study will yield some fascinating data. This will not always be what you expect and not always be in the way that you expect it. As a researcher there is a need to think on your feet and a need, at times, to step back from the research and let your mind go blank. Out of this can arise what Polanyi (1962) called 'tacit knowledge' and such knowledge can point researchers forward out of a stuckness. Such tacit knowledge can often arise in the form of metaphors, images and even dreams about your research.

There are some research approaches that actively embrace the use of creative forms of expression, for example Moustakas' heuristic research (1990), autoethnography (e.g. Etherington, 2004) or narrative research (Speedy, 2008). If we consider heuristics further, its strength lies in its careful and creative working of the researcher's relationship with the research study. Developing this heuristic perspective, which is deeply rooted in reflexivity, is of value to any research project, especially those of a qualitative nature. Moustakas argues persuasively that a research study does not only have to result in a standard research report, but that creative depictions of research findings are valuable, important and useful. This can include poetry and artwork, dance and other forms of performance. Such creativity is not so far away from us in these internet days.

Creativity then can be a key feature of the dissemination of your research findings. It is one thing to battle to get a journal or a conference to accept a paper based on your research study, it is another thing to get people to read your paper. There is room for creativity in producing a conference poster. The potential for using creativity also increases hugely when we begin to think about online dissemination. As ever, the key questions are, 'Who is my intended audience?' and 'How can I best reach them?'

> Creativity is not merely the innocent spontaneity of our youth and childhood; it must also be married to the passion of the adult human being, which is a passion to live beyond one's death. (May, 1975: 31)

Now for those of you who don't desire to represent their findings in the form of an interpretive dance, or view their creative process as an existential statement in the way noted by Rollo May above, there is a more mundane functional side to creativity in research. At the outset of this section, we mentioned some of these areas and we don't wish to revisit these in any depth. The area that we would however like to flag up before finishing is that creating a dissertation (paper, thesis, poster, book, etc.) can be incredibly satisfying. On completion of Chapter 4 this book seems far from complete to us and motivation may begin to wane, but by the time we reach Chapter 9 things are really taking shape and an end product is in sight. Inevitably this end product will have strengths and weaknesses, as we have already touched upon in the first activity within this chapter, but it will still be something to be proud of. Do however be prepared to be relieved, happy and a little bit disappointed at the end of your research journey.

In the spirit of creativity, and bridging from this chapter to the next, one of us (WW) wrote the following:

POEM FOR THE NEW RESEARCHER

You seem to be well provisioned for your journey
With your consent letters and ethical approval forms close to hand
Your study has been passed by the relevant committee

And your instruments are all polished and fit for purpose
Your back-up team waits by their mobes and computers
And the long days of waiting and planning are over.

But now you are on your own
Contact is made and data begins to flow in
You are excited – it's happening at last.

But then a snag arises
You are not getting all of what you expected
You start to feel disappointed, deskilled and downcast
And overwhelmed by paper and computer files
And a data analysis process that seems endless.

And what was your burning question?
And what was so exciting about it?
It's time to step back and let the tacit work begin
It's time for some kind words of encouragement.

You return to your data
Unsure – but true of heart
And patterns begin to emerge
Not always the one you expected or wanted
But telling their own truth and taking you by surprise.

You have a story to tell now
Of what you have found and what it means to us all
And you are older and wiser
And still have unanswered questions
That demand their own journeys in the future.

The student voice: Pariya Habibi

So what were my burning research questions? I always had questions about a lot of things in life but deciding which question was important enough to me to become the title of my Doctoral thesis was not a straightforward task. In fact I remember the first time Clare, our tutor and co-author of this book, actually asked us in class to start capturing a few of the 'burning' research ideas we might have. I remember wondering how I could be sure that my questions were actually important enough for me to constitute what I interpreted as the meaning of 'burning'. Even then, having settled on an area of interest, I still needed to decide which question in these areas proved, not just burning, but 'cool' enough to translate into a feasible research question that I could satisfactorily explore during my time as a trainee counselling psychologist.

The area I was interested to know more about was the nature of burnout for staff working in psychiatric acute settings. This stemmed from my experience working as a junior therapist within a hospital for people who used complex self-harm. There was a lot of research around attachment style (e.g. see Bretherton, 1992) and its role in personality development but little about how it might explain the factors that lead to burnout in those who work in mental health acute units within a caring role. I began to do a literature review that invoked using Google Scholar to search terms like 'staff', 'burnout' and 'acute settings'. There was one paper in particular that caught my attention (Goodwin et al., 2003). In this paper, the authors had actually created a questionnaire to measure how patients housed in an inpatient acute setting felt about their organisation and the staff (known as the Service Attachment Questionnaire). Although this looked at the issue from a different angle, it gave me a starting point.

Meanwhile there seemed little sign of an inventory that could be used as a tool to measure staff's perception and attitude to the organisation they worked in. Such a gap in the literature made me think I could base my research proposal around creating a questionnaire using mixed methods (i.e. both qualitative and quantitative methods) to allow others to begin to explore this area. In this way, I wanted my research to actually make a difference to both patient and staff welfare in mental health acute units. The latter was pertinent to any proposal I have because it gives me the motivation to complete such a project, especially in the field of psychotherapy where research is not always used to inform practice and at a wider level inform the politics of running psychiatric units.

The next part involved doing the fieldwork or problem solving the practicalities of answering this research question I was contemplating. In retrospect, this step was essential to formulating whether a burning idea can translate into an actual research proposal – this is something I would recommend you do even if you are not fully sure whether the question that wanders into your mind about your practice, or someone else's practice, is the burning question. Such a 'litmus' test is vital in making preparations because no matter how 'hot' your question is, it's not a guarantee that it will necessarily form a brilliant research proposal. Such pragmatic thinking has never come naturally to me but speaking to my tutors and peers has helped me with this.

As a result of this fieldwork, I concluded that two main areas needed addressing before I could even begin to formulate the research question. First, in designing a questionnaire I would need a mixture of qualitative and quantitative methods. As a psychology graduate with a mainly quantitative background I had little idea of how these qualitative methods would work in practice and whether I was competent enough single-handedly to analyse the data it would create! Such an obstacle, I quickly realised, could be overcome because there are plenty of papers and textbooks about the process of using qualitative methods in the literature (see Chapter 7 in this book as a starting point) and I was well placed within a excellent research institution with access to a wide range of researchers who had plenty of experience in using qualitative methods. This is another strong word of advice – always look out to the wider network you are in when considering whether to start a research project, because others can bring in something to your project.

The next question I had to tackle, which perhaps is even more important than the first one, was where I would get my participants from. Ideally, based on my literature review, I wanted participants to be representative of different inpatient settings across the region. However, it was unlikely that I could just write to ward managers across different organisations and get their backing to invite their staff to participate in such a project. As the content of the research could be potentially quite delicate, I had to really inform the subjects as to what they were consenting to get involved in (e.g. if I held focus groups in which I explored themes in attachment styles of staff by asking them questions about how they felt about their jobs and the organisation they worked for, it could lead to all sorts of other issues). I would also have to convince managers and the setting's internal research ethics committee, as well as the ethics committee at the University of Manchester, that for staff to give up time to take part in the study would be in some way of benefit to their organisation and the individuals involved too.

Now of course this isn't to say that these questions can't be answered, but you can see the time it would take just to answer them, especially as I had to orally present my proposal to a research assessment panel in less than four months from settling on where my passion was. In other words, time was not on my side and this will apply to any working therapist who has a burning research question and wants to really give their question the time it deserves and not just settle for a crude answer.

So what was the end product of this? That's the bit I'm still figuring out, but I have other pockets of ideas that I can explore which are certainly not too foreign to attachment theory and burnout in mental health staff. In fact, I hope that this overview does not make you think that pragmatism is what often impedes the creativity that drives research. Instead I hope it can show you how the two can feed into each other so that before you decide to commit to the exciting question you have, you know that you have a chance of ending your journey somewhere nearer the 'truth' than where you were before. In conclusion, for me at least, the most important part in doing research almost comes before the research starts.

Summary points

- Critical thinking is essential in counselling and psychotherapy research. Remember that there are always valid counterpoints to all arguments.
- Individuals often have burning questions when considering what research project to undertake. This often needs harnessing to become more specific.
- Choosing a topic that you are passionate enough about is important to see a project through to fruition.
- There are often practical hurdles to undertaking a research project. These might include your own existing skill level, the cost of a training course, the time you have available to undertake the research and the support that backs your efforts.
- Research involves numerous creative processes that spread throughout any project. It is helpful to be prepared to be creative and enjoy breathing life into a piece of research.

FURTHER READING

For critical thinking around counselling and psychotherapy:

Feltham, C. (2010) *Critical Thinking in Counselling and Psychotherapy*. London: Sage.
Wampold, B.E. (2001) 'Contextualizing psychotherapy as a healing practice: culture, history and methods', *Applied and Preventive Psychology*, 10: 69–86.

For passion and creativity:

Etherington, K. (2004) *Becoming a Reflexive Researcher: Using Our Selves in Research*. London: Jessica Kingsley Publishers.
Moustakas, C. (1990) *Heuristic Research: Design, Methodology and Applications*. London: Sage.
Speedy, J. (2008) *Narrative Inquiry and Psychotherapy*. London: Palgrave.

5

The Impact of Undertaking Research on the Researcher

Abstract

This chapter begins a process of reflecting upon the consequences of undertaking research upon those conducting it. During the first half we begin by encouraging the reader to consider their motivations for engaging in a piece of research. Here we examine both the personal and professional motivations for such work. Within the second half of this chapter we then consider the potential impact of the different life stages of a research project on those conducting it. In particular, we break up the research process into the following stages: 1) choosing a research topic; 2) the research proposal and ethical clearance; 3) data generation; 4) data analysis; 5) writing-up; 6) the fallout from dissemination. These different stages are considered in relation to the potential challenges and successes that researchers may encounter. Finally, one of our current trainees, Andrew Greaves, provides a commentary around the resonance they feel to the topics covered in this chapter. Further reading is also provided.

THOUGHT BOX 5

Imagine you are about to undertake a new piece of research

Consider:

- How do you imagine the subject matter might impact upon you?
- How do you imagine the research process might impact upon you?
- What types of support might you need to help you complete the work?

What is the impact of research?

Deciding what to research can be a curious and difficult endeavour. Some people know right from the start what it is they will be looking at, others will take weeks to settle on a subject. In considering where it is that you are going to end up, it is well worth reflecting on why we are undertaking a research study in the first place. For example, we may be researching to gain an academic qualification, because our job demands it, because we have a passion for the topic, because we are committed to a therapeutic method or technique, or a mixture of several of these. Each of these reasons appears regularly within the groups of people that we work with on the courses that we teach.

By the nature of our work as university lecturers a majority of the people we work with are those undertaking research to obtain a qualification. Within this group, there are always individuals who may feel ambivalent about having to do a research project at all (here we would refer back to Chapter 2 and the discussions about the importance of research to therapists). This ambivalence can be compounded further if individuals have chosen a topic that does not particularly interest them. For instance, we generally like research, but we also acknowledge that it can be dull or heavy going at times – think of trying to proofread what you have written, or chasing up some obscure reference that you failed to note down properly at the time, or being surrounded by piles of interview transcripts and not knowing where and how to start your data analysis. If the topic does not especially grip you and the data you get is not that striking and meaningful to you then it will be hard to maintain momentum. With this in mind, it might be worth seeing undertaking research as a creative process, and like all creative moments there are times of high energy and excitement, steady times of getting on with it, and then duller times when you face feelings of 'Why bother?', 'Is it worth it?' or 'Can I do it?' From our perspective, it is also worth holding onto the belief that creative processes also have their eureka moments where things do slot into place.

Some researchers capture these sentiments of frustration and illumination within the research journals that they keep. Some examples from Master's dissertations are noted in Box 1.

BOX 1

Students' experiences of completing research

Gareth Williams, who explored creativity within therapy, asked himself, 'What's the point of me doing this when there are texts out there like the Encyclopaedia of Creativity that have literally thousands of pages exploring a myriad of issues related to creativity?' (Williams, 2010: 37).

Fevronia Christodoulidi, who explored spirituality and culture, wrote in an email to her academic supervisor, included in her dissertation: 'I feel inspired and in deep process; I also feel that all this 'data' is becoming more intense now for a reason and I am not

---

sure how to "grasp" it and how to "use" it later as researcher … How to put it into words?' (Christodoulidi, 2006: 30).

Gillian James, who looked at bereavement issues for Christian clients, using mixed methods – a focus group and a questionnaire – says: 'In spite of her excitement about this subject and the strong desire to know the answers to the questions posed, the researcher did hesitate a long time before embarking on this research. She felt intimidated by her lack of experience in this field, her feeling of helplessness and inadequacy' (James, 2004: 10).

Linda Ankrah says: 'Working in an academic environment has been a challenging task for me … There were times when I wondered if I had bitten off more than I could chew, yet when people began to express an interest in what I was doing I was encouraged' (Ankrah, 2000: 100).

Finally, Susan Pixton writes: 'I originally started this process wanting to inform my own practice and wanting to listen to gay, lesbian and bisexual clients and their affirming experiences of counselling. I have reached the end of this process feeling humbled, moved, privileged, grateful and truly informed' (Pixton, 2002: 119).

In this context it is interesting to consider some research undertaken by Ann Scott (2008) who interviewed six novice researchers who had undertaken Master's studies using heuristic or phenomenological approaches. Scott dramatically recalls the words of one researcher, who was very challenged by undertaking research into eating disorders, as follows: 'I had done all the transcripts and I thought, "Oh God! This is going to consume me. I could feel as if I was going to be swallowed up by it"' (Scott, 2008: 13). Research for counsellors and psychotherapists is therefore often far from emotion free. Interestingly, when considering Thought Box 5 above, in which we ask you to consider what support you might want during a research project, Scott usefully draws a distinction between the rather disinterested academic support offered by the course tutors and the more holistic support and understanding required by the student researchers. Although we hope that tutors are aware and supportive of such processes, peer support networks do seem to be a consistent source of help for a majority of trainees.

Size matters (in quantitative terms)

Many of us do approach counselling research with a passion for a topic. This might be something we really want to find out more about or maybe to prove the utility of a pet technique or approach. A common trap to fall into with quantitative research questions is that it is very easy to get rather grand about all of this. For example, you might want to prove that person-centred therapy is the best therapeutic approach or that psychodynamic therapy is always the most successful with a particular client group. Realistically, as mentioned in the previous chapter, to satisfy such research desires or passions would take a huge amount of human resources – actually a research team – and would take an incredibly long time to do (assuming it was a valid endeavour in the first place). In this case, the sole unfunded researcher therefore has to think more about completing a good, small practice evaluation, rather than over-egging the pudding with the all-singing, all-dancing research project.

The pitfall of aiming too big is also commonplace within qualitative research. For example, people often begin with questions such as 'I want to understand the experience of people who are bereaved who seek counselling', or 'I want to find out what is most helpful for clients.' To do either of these research topics on an appropriate scale inevitably involves small numbers of people otherwise it becomes unmanageable. So again, one is forced to do a small, in-depth study that can tell us something about that particular group of people, which may or may not be generalisable. It is likely that, as mentioned within Chapter 7, the research question would need to be honed to a particular grouping to retain a helpful focus. Finally, if you want to use a mixed methods approach, say using both qualitative and quantitative methods, it will likely get even harder to design a study that is doable within a short enough timespan and with limited resources. This latter area leads to the potential for systematic case studies to become a standard, valid endeavour for the student researcher (see McLeod, 2010).

This scaling-down from the grand passion of the would-be research study to what is actually sensibly doable can be a painful and dispiriting process. There is a real sense of loss involved. Then, in doing the reframed research project, the new researcher finds out that they have to make do and mend with whoever is willing to participate. The numbers willing to join in may prove lower and less interesting than what one had hoped for. From our point of view as research supervisors, there is always an interesting research story to be told even using what initially appears to be unpromising data. Indeed two of us have told the story of a research project that failed, as a warning to other researchers (West and Hanley, 2006). It can be helpful to think about possible interpretations of difficulties in relation to disappointing research responses. For example, is this response a reaction to research design and/or does it tell us something about the topic? For instance, if our topic is in a taboo area it may well be difficult to find research participants.

So there is a necessary letting go of what we hoped to have happen – our grand research ideas get scaled down and there is a need to make sense of, and engage deeply with, what data we have been able to gain from the study we are ultimately left with. Fortunately, it is still relatively early days for counselling research and so, in many areas of practice, a well-designed research project, however small, can still often make a useful contribution. In the activity that follows we hope to get you thinking about the issues tackled in the first section of this chapter. What are your reasons for undertaking a piece of research and are they sufficient to see you through?

ACTIVITY 9: Is your research idea meaningless?

As we introduced in Chapter 2 of this text, research is not currently viewed as a major strand to development as a therapist within Britain. Part of the reason behind this might be because the research that is being undertaken proves of little obvious importance to the wider community. From the other side of the fence, researchers often joke that the higher the esteem of the research journal the fewer readers it has. Interestingly the notion of 'impact' now seems to have some relevance within research communities and there is increasingly an emphasis upon doing meaningful work that has an impact upon the communities they focus upon. Bridging these two worlds to some small degree proves a major hope of this text, and the activity below purposefully gets you thinking about the impact of your work.

This activity attempts to:

1   display the different types of data that quantitative and qualitative questions generate
2   get the reader to consider how their research interests resonate with the broader community (if they do at all)

and

3   encourage the reader to begin reflecting upon the impact that the research may have upon them.

The activity

This begins with a relatively quick activity. Note down, using a scale of 1 to 5 (1 being no connection and 5 being a substantial connection) your personal connection to the research topic that interests you (e.g. is it linked to something that happened to you?). Now move to consider how connected this topic is to your professional interests (e.g. is it linked to your job?) and rate it on the same scale. Before moving on to the second part of this activity, pause for a second and reflect upon your answers – is this quantitative data beginning to give you a sense of what has motivated you to this point?

In parts two and three of the task we then move to getting you to unpack the numbers generated above using qualitative data (for those of you who are interested this could be described as an explanatory mixed methods research design – with the words being used to explain the numbers that have been generated – see Creswell and Plano-Clark, 2011, for more discussion on mixed methods research). Part two asks you to reflect upon what you might get from undertaking the research and also what the broader counselling and psychotherapy community might get from it too. This seems important when considering the notion of impact mentioned above. Finally, for anyone about to engage in a research endeavour, in part three of this exercise it seems essential to ask yourself – 'Is the potential impact, whether personal or professional, sufficient to see you through the work?' and 'Are your desired outcomes for the work really realistic?' In part these questions are likely to be best discussed with someone else (maybe a research supervisor) to challenge you and provide guidance if needed, but this activity can be a good starting place for such discussions. Activity Box 9 summarises this activity.

ACTIVITY BOX 9

Is your research idea meaningless?

Part 1

On a scale of 1–5 (1 = no connection, 5 = a substantial connection) rate the following questions:

- How connected is your research topic to your personal interests?
- How connected is your research topic to your professional interests?

Part 2

Now consider the following qualitative questions:

- What do *you* anticipate getting from your research project?
- What will the profession get from your research project?

Part 3

Finally, consider:

- Is the potential impact of the work, whether personal or professional, sufficient to see you through the work?
- Are your desired outcomes for the work really realistic?

Your findings

If we begin by reflecting upon part one of the activity, what scores did you give each question? Do you have a particular leaning towards developing your professional interests, or are you more inclined to focus in on something that you have a strong personal investment in? In the eventuality that you are not personally or professionally interested in the topic, are you sure you are considering the right topic?

In part two of the activity, where do you stand on the question of output? Is the project really a personal investigation solely for you, or does your interest lie in contributing to the professional community of counsellors and psychotherapists? These issues are not mutually exclusive at all, but if the research had little relevance to the professional community, the question 'Is it really research?' could be asked.

Finally, what are your gut reactions to part three? Have you got a topic that is going to fuel you through the whole piece of work, or are you going to run dry mid-way through? Alternatively, do you really feel that your hopes of the research are attainable, or might you have to scale down your plans a little? Questions such as these are difficult to ascertain without informed guidance, but thinking forward can help shortcut some of these questions with research supervisors (or expensive consultants).

Our findings

In our group work with students this activity provides an incredibly wide spread of responses. Below we have created four themes (see this as a thematic analysis of sorts if you will) that encapsulate the groupings we encounter. In each we discuss the findings related to parts two and three of the activity.

The extremes: one or the other

There is always a contingent of the class who fall into the extremes on our scales. They are solely personally or professionally directed towards a research topic. Both have strengths and weaknesses and often the passion sees the person past the finishing line. In relation to the personal link, some individuals find the process very searching, and the topics link to issues close to their heart (possibly too close). For instance, an individual exploring bereavement might be trying to answer questions that they have about the subject within their own life. In contrast, someone who is solely professionally motivated might complete a project around their working role because their employer is paying for their studies. This might prove convenient, but it could potentially bore the socks off the researcher if they are not truly interested in the topic (fortunately this doesn't occur often).

The slightly ambivalent: a bit of both

For this group the research project is often a task to be completed to obtain the award they are studying for. They are not particularly charged up with the idea of completing the project but they can see it's a useful opportunity to engage in a deeper way with a particular area of interest. This group might begin to waver in energy for the project as it goes on. Alternatively, it might spark an interest as the process develops.

The enthusiastic: a lot of both

This group is likely to be fun to work with. They are so passionate about the project that they live and breathe it during its lifespan. They may also turn up one day with a collection of files thousands of words above the required word count. Completing the dissertation is not likely to be a problem, but there might be a substantial feeling of loss once it is complete! Master's students – beware of the Doctorate bug.

The uninspired: nothing to report

Finally, we should also mention those people who have yet to find a topic. As passionate as tutors are about their own topics, it is very common that some people have still to settle on what it is they want to do. This is particularly relevant to those who have yet to get a grasp on what a research project might look like/consist of. The job of a good tutor will be to support conversations about how glimmers of ideas might be harnessed into doable research projects.

Discussion

Choosing a research topic is never completely straightforward. There are often competing priorities that pull people in different directions. As has been noted in earlier chapters, counsellors and psychotherapists are often reticent about research, and question its relevance to their practice (e.g. see Chapter 2 of this text). In instances where the link between what you do in practice and the research project you undertake is minimal, bridging the divide will therefore become a major challenge. The reflections from undertaking the above activity outline some ways in which this challenge may manifest, with some heading down pathways that prove too personal whilst others become too professional.

If recommendations were to be made from this experience, then aiming for a healthy balance of both personal and professional motivations would be advocated. The personal resonance with a topic appears important to maintain sufficient interest in a topic to see it come to fruition, and the professional interest acts to complement this passion. Whilst we would not advocate undertaking a research project purely for professional reasons, this component provides a useful reminder that research should have an audience of interested others (McLeod, 2003) beyond the researcher him- or herself.

The lifespan of a research project: Challenges and successes

In this section we move on from our general feelings towards research and our motivations for undertaking the research that we do, to consider more explicitly the potential challenges and successes that researchers may face as they work through a project. In Box 2 we outline a number of challenges and successes for each stage. We hope that such content will give you a sense of the relevant tasks for each element of a research project.

BOX 2

The challenges and successes encountered during the lifespan of a research project

1 Choosing a research topic

It is usually not that difficult to come up with a general area of counselling research interest; indeed sometimes there just seems to be too many topics we would like to research. It is good not to rush this process of settling on a research area. It can be fun

---

to read and talk about potential topics. It is interesting to find out what research has been previously done and whether one's proposed topic is in some way a replication of previous research, or whether one is breaking new ground or possibly a mixture of both. There may be good reasons why there are gaps in the research literature so it is worth reflecting on whether one's proposed research is doable within the time and other resources available. There are plenty of gaps still within counselling research, especially in Britain, and research studies from abroad will have relevance but may not be exactly replicable here.

2 The research proposal and ethical clearance

Producing a good-enough research proposal may seem a hard slog but it is actually a very useful experience. Putting your preliminary thinking about your research topic down on paper is essential for harnessing your project. It also makes the final write-up of the research so much easier. It allows you to become aware of possible problems and challenges and gives you and your supervisor some confidence that the research is doable and likely to produce useful findings.

The process of ethical clearance can feel like a bit of a bind at times – this is where you have to dot the 'i's and cross the 't's of the design that you have put together. As a starting point it can be helpful to find out who is likely to be on the committee and to do your research about the process (e.g. whether it is university, NHS or other protocols – each have their own nuances). This will give you more confidence in dealing with the committee and knowing what they want from you. It will also shorten the time involved.

Although the nuts and bolts of ethical clearance can be challenging, thinking about ethics is a very necessary part of any research process involving humans. Furthermore, the care required in gaining ethical approval can be a useful form of ethical consciousness raising. Such awareness is part of counsellor training with regard to self and clients so it should be relatively easy to transfer these understandings to the research process. Thinking through possible ethical dilemmas is good practice and they do arise in research on a regular basis. For example, in more exploratory forms of research, the questions asked within a research interview are likely to evolve and change over time (Kvale and Brinkman, 2009) so issues around informed consent need to be carefully addressed and revisited.

3 Data generation

This rarely works out as hoped for. In quantitative research, you might not get the number of surveys filled in that you hoped for. You can of course send reminders and hopefully get a few more, but this can raise anxieties. You may then begin to wonder how few you need for statistical tests and significance. As there are so many surveys around these days you might want to consider how yours is special (to your potential participants), or at least user friendly.

(Continued)

(Continued)

It is also typical to have many promising offers for participation in qualitative interviews or focus groups but then to find that the practicalities seem to get in the way. Arranging the time and place for a focus group can seem all but impossible, and the huge number of possible interview participants seems to shrink alarmingly when you start to try and arrange dates. Do not take it personally, it just matters less to them than it does to you! So aim to recruit more possible participants than you need. If you do find that you have more potential participants than you need, be thankful!

4 Data analysis

This can be painful. We are struck by how often most of us put off this stage, especially if it is qualitative. It is best to try and clear some full days and throw yourself into it! Again what the data shows will likely be different to what you had hoped for. Can you let go of what you wanted and engage with what the data has to tell you, qualitative or quantitative? This is where a good pilot will have been helpful in alerting you to what the data might be like.

5 Writing up

This can feel like a mountain to climb, but staying with that metaphor you go one step at a time until you reach the summit. A good research proposal is often a good framework for writing up. Also, if you have kept a research diary then you will have plenty of notes that can help in writing up (if you have not begun one, you could still start at this stage to capture ongoing thoughts). Also, bring your knowledge of your habits when writing to this process. For example, some people like to sketch everything out before any formal writing; others like to write a whole chunk and then edit it. Use whatever has worked for you previously and give yourself plenty of time to devote to this task. One tip however would be that several clear days are usually better than working in smaller chunks over a longer period of time!

6 The fallout from dissemination

It is good to share what you have found. In fact, it could be argued that you have an ethical responsibility to use the information that people have very kindly contributed. With this in mind, it can be helpful, with your supervisor's support, to choose your intended audience(s). This can be opportunistic, taking advantage of a timely but relevant conference, workshop or special edition of a journal. Think about who you most want/need to know about your research. Do however be mindful that you may well not get the response you expected, and this can be difficult to hear at times. However, in a similar way, you might also get unexpected responses that tell you something different and useful.

If you have written a piece for an academic qualification, do take note of examiners/report readers who give strong positive feedback. Do think seriously about dissemination. It can feel like a step too far, or even a scary step, but if you have found out something that is valuable then you owe it to your participants (and to yourself) to pass your findings on. (For the lecturers reading this text, we encourage you to consider offering to co-author a paper. Such support can prove mutually beneficial to all involved.)

ACTIVITY 10: Preventing research failure?

Within therapy, the idea that we can prevent 'failure' by bringing to the fore discussions about the therapeutic process is receiving more attention (e.g. Cooper and McLeod, 2010; Lambert, 2011). The same principle applies to this activity. In the section above we have discussed potential issues that might arise throughout the lifespan of the research project, and here we hope to get you to personalise this process. Our hope is to heighten your own awareness of the pitfalls that you might encounter with a view to doing something about them.

This activity attempts to:

1   once again, display the different types of data that quantitative and qualitative questions generate
2   consider what research tasks the reader is likely to struggle with during the lifespan of a research project

and

3   encourage the reader to consider strategies that they may use for overcoming the challenges they face when conducting research.

The activity

With the above aim in mind, we ask that you consider the same stages noted in Box 2 above in relation to your own research processes: 1) choosing a research topic; 2) the research proposal and ethical clearance; 3) data generation; 4) data analysis; 5) writing-up; 6) the fallout from dissemination. These might be projects that you are completing (or contemplating completing) in your workplace or as student projects. Initially, rate them out of 10, with 10 meaning that you envisage struggling with the process.

Following on from this rating process we then ask that you reflect upon why you might struggle in the areas that you scored above 5. Note these thoughts down and then take a step back and imagine taking on a supportive role for a friend. If they were struggling with their studies in the way you describe, what advice might you give them? Once again note this down but this time keep it in a safe place – your words of wisdom may come in handy at some point during your own process. If this does prove to be the case, you can follow the instruction articulated in part four of Activity Box 10: 'Listen to your own words of wisdom.'

ACTIVITY BOX 10

Preventing research failure?

Part 1

Rate the following research stages from 1 to 10 (1 means that you envisage being able to complete it easily, 10 means that you are going to struggle a lot with it).

1 Choosing a research topic
2 The research proposal and ethical clearance
3 Data generation
4 Data analysis
5 Writing up
6 The fallout from dissemination

Part 2

For any item you rate above 5 note down why you feel you might struggle.

Part 3

Finally, for each of the struggles you have recorded, consider them to be the thoughts of a friend. What advice would you give them on each of the points?

Part 4

Listen to your own words of wisdom.

Your findings

Here we would be very interested to hear which areas you identify as potential pitfalls. Did a particular area stand out as one that you feel you will struggle with? Were there areas that you felt you would have no difficulty with at all (or at least viewed them as some of the less daunting processes)? Finally, when considering the advice you would give, did it sound helpful?

Our findings

Now, it's not possible to go through each of the questions in turn, but through our experience of supervising students, it's notable that there is no one area that people struggle with more than others. Within each cohort of students there will be those that find it difficult in the early stages, those who hit brick walls mid-way through, and those who need a shove over the finishing line. In fact, during our own training and subsequent research, these phases still cause all three of the authors major headaches.

In turn here are some of the pieces of advice that have helped us with our own work (some of these might be multipurpose, but for simplicity's sake we've attributed the advice under one heading only).

1 Choosing a research topic
   o   'You should talk to your supervisor about that bit.'
   o   'You should remember you've got to live with it for quite some time.'
2 The research proposal and ethical clearance
   o   'Keep it simple – you should not try to overcomplicate things.'
   o   'You should be ready to make some changes before beginning the research.'
3 Data generation
   o   'You should stop procrastinating and just do it.'
   o   'Why don't you just ask them if they will take part?'
4 Data analysis
   o   'It's not that important really. You should take it less seriously.'
   o   'You should look in the handbook.'
5 Writing-up
   o   'You should break it down into bite-size chunks.'
   o   'It is really important that you finish this. The participants (and you) have invested so much into it.'
6 The fallout from dissemination
   o   'What do they know anyway? You know it's a good piece of work.'
   o   'Maybe they have a point and you should listen to it.'

Discussion

We hope you now have a good sense of what you may be getting yourself into and what the consequences of undertaking such a piece of work might be. It is likely that you will be at least slightly daunted by a number of these phases. This seems a very normal response to what is a challenging process – as indicated earlier in this chapter, all of the authors of this book still encounter significant hurdles in the research projects that we undertake. We also do not imagine that it is possible to pre-empt every potential pitfall, but hopefully by undertaking this activity you will have identified the areas that you might associate with the biggest headaches.

Although identifying where your research project might struggle is an important part of Activity 10, probably more important is considering how you might overcome these challenges. In being proactive we hope that you might have begun to identify what it is that you can do to nip some of these difficulties in the bud (or at least to have a sense of what you might do about them if they do arise). Importantly, we feel that it is essential to remember that you are unlikely to be alone in undertaking a research project. There will be interested others in student groups, professional communities and families, and do not forget your research supervisor (or consultant if you are not undertaking it as part of a training programme). Just as you would discuss challenges within your therapeutic practice with others, why not do the same within your research?

The student voice: Andrew Greaves

In reading this chapter and being a trainee myself, it certainly provided me with some insightful points as to what to expect in the future as my research progresses, but also provided a great comfort to read that previous feelings about undertaking research as a whole were perfectly normal. Briefly, in the following paragraphs I will share my own response to the chapter, drawing on my own experience, which will hopefully provide you with a more personal account of the impact of undertaking research.

I shall aptly start at the beginning of the research process by referring to Activity 9: Is your research idea meaningless? I feel (in my opinion) that this is the most important question you can ever ask yourself in starting research. The three parts referred to in the activity seem to encompass each conversation I have had with my fellow students on the Doctorate in Counselling Psychology, and still do so. I remember asking, 'Why am I doing this work?', which seems to be echoed throughout the chapter. On a personal note, I found the creation of my question a very difficult process and it did raise a lot of doubts in the areas that have been mentioned (passion, attainability, size, knowledge, contribution, etc.). It is something that should not be taken lightly. These initial stages do, unfortunately, provide quite a headache, but as I discussed with my tutor, it is far better to realise the error of your ways in the first few weeks and months of searching the literature, than in the middle of gathering your data! Interestingly, in preparation for having your research proposal assessed or attempting to obtain ethical clearance, it seems that most of my colleagues' questions (including mine) have changed somewhat from our initial ideas, providing a clear example of the flexibility and patience required in doing work such as this. I think that the poignant point which I take away from the first half of the chapter is that there needs to be a balancing act of personal passion (doing what you want to do) and professional pragmatism (being able to do what you want to do) to make the inevitable moments of anxiety and frustration few and far between.

When looking upon the title of the chapter – 'The impact of undertaking research on the researcher' – I have to think about how I feel, as I am the researcher in question. Unfortunately, I can only provide a limited view as I have not yet completed the research journey and still have many challenges and successes to get through. Currently, however, it seems that undertaking research is both exciting, as I am providing the counselling community with new knowledge, but very intimidating, as I am the one finding said knowledge, and just how does the amount of research and data I have on my desk translate into a coherent piece of literature? However, I'm sure that in reading this book, you will be provided with some useful insights on just how to do that.

In reading through the chapter several times I think that it provides you, the reader, with comprehensive activities on how to reduce the negative impact that research might have on a personal level, but unfortunately none of these are fail-safe. I think an important question to ask yourself is 'How am I going to react if (or when) something unexpected goes wrong?' I do appreciate that beginning to be aware of where you may falter is useful, but unpredictability resides within the nature of the beast. Something that may not have crossed your mind may suddenly impact a huge proportion of your work, and it is only you who can decide how ferociously it may personally affect you. Is it a motivation to overcome, or more a feeling of waving the white flag of defeat? It was once said to me that completing research is just like being in a relationship. Ups and downs are bound to happen and most of them are unexpected as it is impossible to plan for every eventuality, but it is how you react to these moments that dictates the outcome of your long-term commitment. For these unnerving moments, again, I can only echo the sentiments already stated in this chapter, but I hope it may resonate with you more, coming from a person who is actually doing what is being written about. You really are not alone, and peer support is something that I cannot emphasise enough. Successes or failures, it is important you share and learn from each other because the chances are that if you are feeling a bit wobbly the person sitting beside you will be in the same position.

Summary points

- Undertaking a research project is likely to have a significant impact upon the person doing it.
- The motivation for undertaking research might be personal or professional. It is recommended that a balance of the two is aimed for when choosing a direction for a project.
- Six potential stages that individuals might encounter difficulties are: 1) choosing a research topic; 2) the research proposal and ethical clearance processes; 3) data generation; 4) data analysis; 5) writing-up; 6) the fallout from dissemination.
- It is likely that difficulties will arise and everyone will struggle in different areas.
- Prevention of research failure is better than a cure. Where possible those undertaking research should attempt to plan ahead for pitfalls that they may encounter in their projects.
- Research supervision can be an important source of support when navigating the trials and tribulations of undertaking research.

FURTHER READING

Curiously there is not much literature and even less research literature relating the impact of undertaking research. Some useful resources include:

Moustakas, C. (1990) *Heuristic Research: Design, Methodology and Applications*. London: Sage.
Scott, A. (2008) 'The effect of doing qualitative research on novice researchers', *European Journal for Qualitative Research in Psychotherapy*, 3: 10–18.
Silvester, A. (2011) 'Doing a Doc! – The thoughts, experiences and relationships of students undertaking a Professional Doctorate in Counselling', *Counselling and Psychotherapy Research*, 11 (3): 179–85.

6

Quantitative Research: Collecting and Making Sense of Numbers in Therapy Research

Abstract

Engaging with numbers is often one of the most feared aspects to research that counsellors and psychotherapists report. This chapter therefore aims to offer a gentle introduction to a type of research that can instil some with fear but provide a wealth of riches to others. We begin by considering what quantitative research is, before reflecting upon the storylines that people tell with numbers. After getting you to reflect upon your own relationship with this type of work, we outline some common rationales for undertaking quantitative research and the methods that individuals use (e.g. questionnaires and observations). Some key terms that you might encounter are then presented before introducing some common methods of quantitative data analysis. We then get you to generate some quantitative data, reflecting upon how you are progressing through this book, and consider some of the complexities of mixing quantitative and qualitative research. Finally, Aaron Sefi, an ex-Master's student and counselling service manager, provides a thought-provoking reflection on the chapter. Further reading is also provided.

> **THOUGHT BOX 6**
>
> **How do you *feel* about using numbers in research?**
>
> Consider:
>
> - Do you feel that numbers have a place in counselling and psychotherapy research?
> - How do you feel about using questionnaires in your practice?
> - Do you feel comfortable making sense of numbers?

Overview: what is quantitative research?

The term 'quantitative research' refers to any type of research that summarises concepts into categories that can be counted. These might include measuring the level of risk perceived during an assessment meeting, the strength of the therapeutic relationship or the amount of change that someone indicates whilst in therapy. Within the counselling and psychotherapy research literature, quantitative methods hold an important place, and such methods provide an incredibly useful shorthand for people to reflect upon the complex processes that we are engaged in. Such a view of the world is, however, fraught with complexities and it does not sit well with everyone, a factor that we will consider later on in this chapter.

Two of the most common types of quantitative research are 1) the survey, and 2) the experiment. The first of these is probably very familiar to you and it is likely that you will have completed a survey at some point in your life (possibly about your therapeutic work, but also in other areas of your life). Such a method 'provides a quantitative or numeric description of trends, attitudes, or opinions of a population by studying a sample of that population' (Creswell, 2003: 153). Thus survey designs can prove great at getting a sense of the prevalence of something (e.g. what proportion of schools in Scotland have counselling services), how people are presently behaving (e.g. providing a snapshot of the number of integrative psychotherapists there are in the UK), or how individuals might respond to particular stimuli (e.g. how likely are people with counselling qualifications to apply for jobs in the NHS).

The idea of an experiment might seem further away from the work that you do on an everyday basis. These types of projects aim to 'test the impact of a treatment (or an intervention) on an outcome, controlling for all other factors that might influence that outcome' (Creswell, 2003: 154). It is however quite likely that such research designs have some influence upon your work. For instance, many of the commissioning bodies are likely to utilise such work to provide direction to their decisions. Increasingly there is a move towards evidence-based practices (also termed empirically supported treatments), which are assessed using hierarchies of evidence that place great value upon experimental designs (see Sackett, 1996). Figure 1 provides a summary of the commonly used levels of evidence – those towards the top of the pyramid are viewed as stronger pieces of evidence. Such a model proves contentious due to assumptions of what 'good' research is (e.g. Westen et al., 2004), but whether we agree or disagree with such a conceptualisation, it is difficult to escape the utility in such a framework in clinical decision-making.

The commonly held hierarchy of evidence has bought into a rhetoric which argues that psychological science can follow the same rules as natural science. For some this proves akin to *the* truth. For others, however, the numbers have to be viewed with more caution and considered pragmatically. In particular, it might be more accurate to discuss the way that convincing stories which are told with numbers, rather than presenting them as definitive conclusions. Such a sentiment leads us neatly to our next section.

Figure 1 Levels of evidence

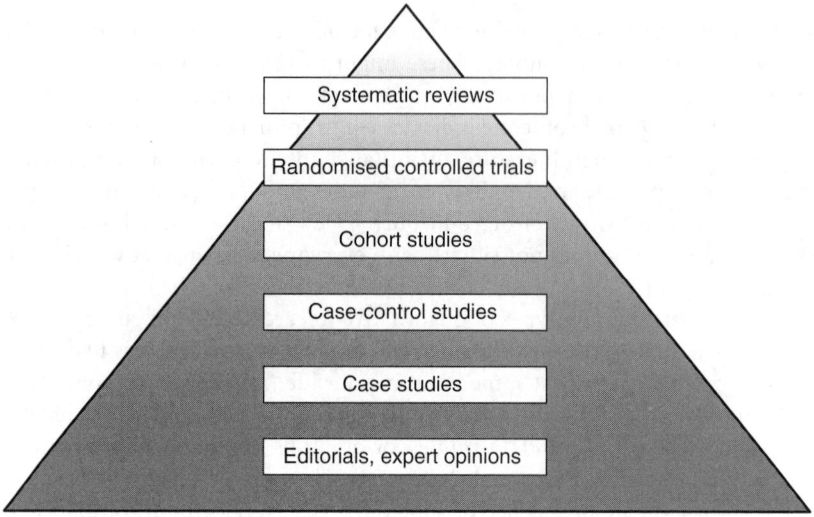

The stories in numbers

At this stage we want you to consider the type of stories that people tell with numbers. In doing so the territory of youth counselling is considered as an example. So let's begin by considering whether such practice works. In framing this as a research question (RQ), we might state:

> **RQ1:** 'Will self-report outcome measures indicate reductions in psychological distress following a period of counselling?'

Thus, it might seem logical to ask the client to complete a measure of wellbeing/distress at the beginning (pre) and at the end of therapy (post) to see if any change occurs. If the results indicated a positive change this might produce a graph such as the one indicated in Graph 1 below.

So ask yourself, is this a convincing storyline? True, it allows us to compare the trajectory of therapy with other studies such as Mick Cooper's (2009) review of literature in this area. It does however raise the question, 'How do we know that this improvement in wellbeing did not just occur by chance?' and thus, 'How can we assert that it was the therapy that had this effect?' The simple answer is that we can't, and this is a weak study. We may therefore add in another measure at the waiting list. This additional measure will provide an indicator of how much progress has gone on before the period of therapy and thus enable us to compare the two time periods. Graph 2 once again displays what you might hope for in such a study, with the waiting period showing little improvement whilst the intervention period showed more change.

Graph 1 A possible potential trajectory of a successful pre to post counselling study

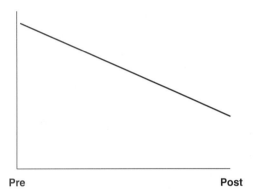

Pre   Post

We're on to a winner now surely? Without a doubt we've created a compelling story and a good research design. It's also a design that is achievable for many services and individuals. However, if you go down this pathway, a rigorous research design is not always enough to influence policy at a high level. Here we would refer to a piece of work that one of us was involved in, exploring the effectiveness of person-centred counselling (Gibbard and Hanley, 2008). It used this type of design with approximately 380 individuals (with a low drop-out rate for this type of study too) and showed very positive results. It will not, however, be considered by the likes of NICE because it does not comply with the hierarchy of evidence they use to assess good research (see above). So what can we do to improve the design to have an impact?

Graph 2 A possible potential trajectory of a two-stage project

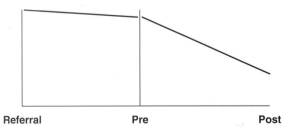

Referral   Pre   Post

We could use more measures to account for any effects due to the instruments used, or we could include a follow-up period to see if change is sustained, or we could get an informed observer (such as a referring teacher) to complete a questionnaire as well (see Graph 3 for what a combination of the latter two of these three points might look like if summarised in graph form). Once again, these would indeed create strong designs, but would they be good enough? Realistically the answer is NO, and the main factor would be that it is not a randomised controlled trial!

Graph 3   A possible potential trajectory of a three-stage project using self and observer report questionnaires

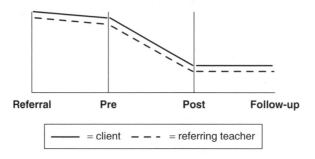

So what is a randomised controlled trial (RCT)? In Mick Cooper's very handy glossary of research terms, he describes it as:

> An experimental study in which participants are randomly assigned to two or more groups, such that the efficacy of the different interventions can be identified. (Cooper, 2008: 186)

Thus, unlike the stories told above, RCTs are not real-world interventions: 1) those involved are assigned to randomly allocated groups (e.g. an intervention group and a non-intervention group or comparison group); and 2) as many factors as possible are controlled for (e.g. people with similar presenting issues are recruited and, to ensure that all participants receive a standard intervention, sessions are often recorded and assessed by independent researchers to check they adhere to common descriptions of the therapy in question). A comparison of the group that receives the intervention and those who receive nothing (or an alternative) can then be made and conclusions drawn as to which is the most effective. There are obviously a lot more nuances to such designs than this, but essentially this encapsulates the ethos of the RCT.

Hopefully our brief overview of some of the stories that people tell with quantitative findings will help to convey some of the complexities and debates within quantitative research. We also hope that the simple graphs we have presented here also give you an idea of how a picture can summarise a thousand words into an easily digestible format. We now return to the basics.

ACTIVITY 11: Do you like numbers in research?

As outlined above, counsellors and psychotherapists often hold strong opinions about quantitative methods of research design. Whether these are positive or negative, it is important to understand the important roles that they can play in research and practice. For instance, you *will* be collecting numbers as part of your work, whether it is simple facts, such as the number of people who attended sessions, or more formalised outcome measures. With this in mind, you may also be glad to know that there are relatively simple methods of making some sense of this data, some of which are outlined later in this chapter. But, at this point, how do you feel about numbers?

This activity attempts to:

1   introduce you to two methods of quantitative data collection
2   help you to understand the use of open and closed questions in data collection

and

3   help you to consider the strengths and weaknesses of each of the above.

The activity

Some of you will be old enough to remember 'Run Around' with Mike Reid, a 1970s teatime game show where a question was presented to a group of children and they were asked to 'run around' to the station that they thought provided the correct answer. We sometimes use the following activity in a sort of 'run around' way by creating a 'human questionnaire' and pinning scales to the wall as answers to the questions posed, and inviting people to stand next to the number or answer that best suits their position. It adds another dimension to the activity – watching people physically squirm in their adoption of a number that does not necessarily fit completely with their opinion! On a more serious level this squirming helps individuals to develop their critical voice in relation to research and questionnaire design. So, in a similar way, we invite you to play 'psychological run around' with us.

Imagine that you have to attach yourself to one of the given points on the scale offered below in response to each of the first two questions offered. To what extent do these positions hold any truth for you? What are the problems in the validity of the answers that you provide? We then open the question out, and invite you to consider the complexities of answering this question in a more open-ended way.

ACTIVITY BOX 11

Answer the following questions:

1   Do you like numbers in research?

Yes/No

(Continued)

(Continued)

2   On a scale of 1–5 rate how much you like numbers in research (1 = not at all, 5 = you like a lot).

1   2   3   4   5

3   How do you feel about numbers?

Your findings

In your game of 'run around' what were your reactions to putting yourself in a particular position?

Let's take the first question. Do you like numbers in research? How strongly did you react? Did you feel yourself wanting to say that you hate numbers, they frighten you, they lead to complicated language in research, and don't fit with the ways that you view your practice? Or did you respond, well it depends by what you mean by the term 'in research' – for instance, if I'm booking a holiday I might well look at TripAdvisor ratings and find them really quite helpful? Or did you wonder if we were talking about your use of numbers in a more systematic research project? Maybe you were thinking about your own particular, looming dissertation? If this is the case, we guess that thoughts about this task may have swayed your response. You might not like using them, and the language of quantitative research might be uncomfortable to you, but you realise they have a political currency so you need to get to like them. Maybe this in turn would provide your dissertation with a greater currency too. Or perhaps you like them because they give a much-needed clarity to the field of psychotherapy and counselling that is useful given the inherently murky world that we operate in.

What about if we open out the question into the Likert scale attached to the second question – how did you respond to that? Did you find yourself actively moving away from the polarised position of 1 or 5, resulting in the 'safe' option of a 3? If so, to what extent does that capture your feelings accurately? Three might mean something like 'not bothered', but that might not be the case at all – you might just feel as though you don't fit too neatly into the other categories that have something rather more definitive to say.

I imagine question three might have felt more comfortable to you in generating fuller data and, because it is likely to fit into your rather more qualitative approach to life (a potentially provocative assumption), we will leave discussion of it here and return to numbers!

Our findings

We now present some of the reflections that our trainees share with us. As outlined earlier, in class we present this activity as a human questionnaire and ask people to move themselves to an adopted position on a scale, which leads to some interesting debate as outlined below.

When presented with a closed question such as 'Do you like numbers in research?', students at first object to being forced into a camp. We rather enjoy the process of making them make a decision as it develops the critical edge to their discussions in relation to formulation and clarity of questions and questionnaire/interview design. It is interesting too that often trainees will hang onto the edge of the group that respond 'yes' because they are not wholly in the yes camp, but there is nowhere else to go. This questions the validity of the findings reached and the extent to which a number can capture the reality of the phenomenon under investigation. We do find, however, that when invited to position themselves on a Likert scale (e.g. a rating scale of 1 to 5), respondents often fall into the normal-distribution, bell-shaped curve, where most respondents fall into the middle section, with fewer falling as outliers on the 1s and 5s, the extreme parts of the scale.

Like you, our trainees often query what we mean by each of the questions raised, suggesting that any meaningful outcomes from the data generated are negated by the lack of clarity and definition. There are also interesting dynamics that take place in the group, where there is some peer pressure to say you don't like numbers, or alternatively kudos attached to those who dare to say they like numbers and are not phased by them. This leads to useful discussions regarding the social desirability and the political context to data and research, issues that are considered further below.

Discussion

I (CL) have a friend who thinks that I think too much. We once went out for a Chinese banquet, at the end of which he went to the table and came back with soup for desert. 'Interesting choice', said I. 'It's just chicken soup Clare!' said he. I use this little anecdote as a vehicle on which to hang further discussion in relation to the activity above.

Defining variables: is it just chicken soup?

In order to take a quantitative approach, we have to be very clear about the phenomena we are rating if the numbers are to mean anything. This is often referred to as operationalising our terms or variables. Pinning variables down is a complex thing, for instance 'Can something ever just be chicken soup?!' In the scenario above, chicken soup to me is Heinz chicken soup; this was chicken and sweetcorn soup. Come to think of it, given the time in which it was presented in the meal we could justifiably have called it pudding! On a more serious level, in the world of counselling and therapy, pinning down variables is inherently difficult. I once tried to name and measure the ingredients of work in a personal development group, only to find that more explorative, qualitative measures were much more helpful in trying to understand the phenomenon under investigation (see Lennie, 2007). Some things, it seems, just can't be pinned down in the way that quantitative analyses demand.

If it is just chicken soup, how successfully might we measure things?

If we are indeed able to reach some sort of consensus regarding the thing we are looking at, then we might be able to, with some sort of meaning, attach scales to the variables under investigation. This has been the case in trying to understand what is going on in cognitive therapy using the Revised Cognitive Therapy Scale (CTS-R: Blackburn et al., 2001) and more recently in the world of person-centred work with the Person-Centred and Experiential Psychotherapy Scale (PCEPS: Elliott, Freire and Westwell, 2011). One might imagine that the philosophical underpinnings of cognitive therapy make such measurement somewhat easier to establish, whereas pinning down the elements of person-centred therapy might be much more troublesome. Take a look at the following in Box 3 as examples.

BOX 3

Two examples from rating scales used to assess the fidelity of therapeutic interventions

Person-Centred and Experiential Psychotherapy Scale v. 10.5 (01/03/11)

PC8. GENUINENESS

How much does the therapist respond in a way that genuinely and naturally conveys their moment-to-moment experiencing of the client? E.g., How much does the therapist sound phony, artificial, or overly professional, formal, stiff, pedantic or affected vs. genuine, idiosyncratic, natural or real?

1   No genuineness: Therapist sounds very fake or artificial.
2   Minimal genuineness: Therapist sounds somewhat wooden, stiff or technical.
3   Slight genuineness: Therapist sounds a bit distant or affected.
4   Adequate genuineness: Therapist sounds natural and unaffected.
5   Good genuineness: Therapist sounds very natural or genuine.
6   Excellent genuineness: Therapist sounds completely genuine, very real or idio-syncratically present, without any façade or pretence.

Or, a similar example from the Cognitive Therapy Scale – Revised (CTS-R):

ITEM 5 – INTERPERSONAL EFFECTIVENESS

Key features: The patient is put at ease by the therapist's verbal and non-verbal (e.g. listening skills) behaviour. The patient should feel that the core conditions (i.e. warmth, genuineness, empathy and understanding) are present. However, it is important to keep professional boundaries. In situations where the therapist is extremely interpersonally effective, he/she is creative, insightful and inspirational.

Three features need to be considered:

i Empathy – the therapist is able to understand and enter the patient's feelings imaginatively and uses this understanding to promote change.

ii Genuineness – the therapist has established a trusting working relationship.

iii Warmth – the patient seems to feel liked and accepted by the therapist.

Rating

0 Therapist's manner and interventions make the patient disengage and become distrustful and/or hostile (absence of/or excessive i, ii, iii).

1 Difficulty in showing empathy, genuineness and warmth.

2 Therapist's style (e.g. intellectualisation) at times impedes his/her empathic understanding of the patient's communications.

3 The therapist is able to understand explicit meanings of patient's communications, resulting in some trust developing. Some evidence of consistencies in sustaining relationship.

4 The therapist is able to understand the implicit, as well as the explicit, meanings of the patient's communications, and demonstrates it in his/her manner. Minor problems evident (e.g. inconsistent).

5 The therapist demonstrates very good interpersonal effectiveness. Patient appears confident that he/she is being understood, which facilitates self-disclosure. Minimal problems.

6 Highly interpersonally effective, even in the face of difficulties.

We have used both of these scales as a vehicle to help us assess our trainees' fitness to practise. Without going into a lengthy discussion, the attaching of a number to the therapeutic 'competencies' defined is a complex business that leads to some helpful and enlightening discussion regarding what is 'good' therapeutic practice. Indeed, how these quantitative measures are used, who they are collated for and what their purpose is lead us into the final section of this discussion.

What are the numbers for?

We touched upon the issue of social desirability earlier in this section. Essentially, we often say what we think we ought to say in a questionnaire. If we use the above tools as some sort of fitness-to-practise measure, will the trainees just show us work that they feel demonstrates a 6 on the CTS-R or PCEPS? We personally feel the quality of the discussion around the number to be the greatest determinant of our trainees' fitness to practise and we make this clear to them at the start of the activity. But what happens to the client who fills in outcome measures regarding the effectiveness of therapy with you, and how valid might their responses be? For instance, if you introduce a measure whilst you are sitting with them, how comfortable might they feel in suggesting that therapy has been of no particular use in alleviating their distress? Furthermore, if the questionnaire is completed whilst sitting alongside clients, is this information utilised explicitly as part of the therapy? Finally, how are these numbers used by your service managers, and how does that impact on your client work? These are not simple questions to answer and we present them hoping to convey some of the complexities inherent in quantitative research. Without a doubt, and as suggested at the opening of this chapter, important stories can be told with numbers, but we do however have to be mindful of using them in a critically informed way.

Doing quantitative research

We now turn to the nuts and bolts of quantitative research. In particular we reflect upon some of the underlying considerations of the use of numbers, the ways that we might collect numbers and the methods of making sense of what we collate.

Numbers provide a shorthand in research. If you ever feel so inclined to further your studies and do a PhD or complete a Doctoral thesis, you will be required to undergo an oral examination of your work, or viva voce, where you are asked to defend the work contained in your thesis. One of the opening questions that you are likely to be asked is, 'So, what are the headlines in this research project?' Numbers provide a clear way of being able to articulate your findings.

If our numbers are sufficiently large we are able to make some type of statistical inferences about the data we obtain in terms of the patterns, trends, differences or relationships in the data sets. The extent to which we are able to do this is dependent on the types of data we have collected. An example might help here. It would be unwise to try to make any particularly definitive statements from data collated using the PCEPS forms owing to the complexities of the statements under investigation, as outlined above. The scale is very useful as a vehicle for discussion, but we would be unwise to say trainee X is significantly more genuine than trainee Y due to their levels on the scale; the numbers are not water-tight or definitive enough to make such a comment. Rather more 'water-tight' or higher-level data, from which we can begin to make these inferences, is referred to as parametric data. This is data where the gaps between each item on the scale are equal (money, time, temperature are all examples). Think, for example, of a tape measure and how useless it would be if you could stretch it. We can always be confident that a centimetre on my tape measure will be the same as a centimetre on Terry's tape measure (although a stretchy one sounds attractive in that I could make my waist any size I wanted!). Because of the certainty of the scale, it means that we are able to apply powerful parametric tests upon the data to help us understand patterns, differences and relationships. These higher levels of data are referred to as interval and ratio data as the gaps between the intervals are equal.

Such definitive numbers are often not available in the world of therapy so we fall into a slightly lower level of numerical data (see for example the type of data collated using CTS-R and PCEPS). This sort of data still allows for statistical tests to be applied but, due to the rather more elastic nature of the rating scale, the tests are not as strong, and are referred to as non-parametric. I often think of parametric tests as highly skilled wine tasters who are able to pin down the wine that they taste to not only a specific region, but to the actual grape variety and valley. I, however, am rather more like a non-parametric test and can just about work out the difference between red and white; well OK – possibly sweet white and very dry …! Levels of data upon which these tests are carried out are referred to as ordinal (where an order or rating is inferred as in the PCEPS example, but where the gaps between each point on the rating scale are not equal) or where people's data is categorised into groups, for example Yes and No in the first question you engaged with above about whether you like numbers in research.

The application of such statistical approaches leads to a clarity of articulating our research outcomes and inherently the data analysis holds, behind the scenes, an audit trail that adds to its validity and reliability. If William inputs a set of numbers into SPSS (originally, Statistical Package for the Social Sciences, but more commonly known by its initials) and I do too then we will both achieve the same result. The audit trails required in qualitative analysis are just as important (if not more so) in order to establish the validity of the findings and conclusions obtained (such issues are considered elsewhere in this text).

Quantitative approaches require particular methods to the design of a study, such as the designs outlined at the start of this chapter. Now that we have considered some of the underlying principles of this type of research we move onto the nuts and bolts of data generation and analysis.

Collecting numbers in therapy research: data generation

Let's imagine that you have identified a question that you want to try to answer for a small research project. Your first job is to think about how you are going to collect the information in order to answer the question. We begin this section by considering the use of questionnaires and surveys, along with a consideration of their strengths and weaknesses, before moving on to the use of observations and how they might be incorporated into a quantitative design.

Questionnaires and surveys

We are all probably very familiar with this method of data collection, and are probably aware too of its limitations! How many times have you walked through town and actively avoided somebody with a clipboard and pen who clearly wanted to ask some questions of you? One of the advantages of the use of questionnaires and surveys is that they potentially allow for a large population of people to be questioned; however, the response rate is often very small in terms of return. Questionnaires and surveys are widely used in counselling and psychotherapy in trying to understand what is going on in therapy and in understanding the professional context of counselling. They are attractive to researchers in terms of the potential large participant pool that might be accessed, but also in terms of the ease with which quantitative data might be analysed in terms of the inclusion of closed questions (answered by Yes or No) or the attaching of some sort of rating scale. Qualitative data from more open questions that might be included can also be coded to allow us to count up the number of times that participants refer to a particular theme in their open-ended answers, so allowing for a quantitative analysis to be undertaken.

Return rates for questionnaires can be problematically low. Issues of social desirability can make us question the validity of our findings and, where we include open-ended questions to invite comment, limited data might be included. Our answers might be limited by the mood in which we find ourselves or the social context in which we complete the measure. On a more basic level, human beings have limited attention spans. If questionnaires are too lengthy, responses may be minimal and it is not unusual to see participants forming a response set where they notice a direction to the questions and circle the same number throughout the questionnaire. Reverse-scoring questions can often be helpful in these cases where some questions are positively framed and some negatively and the scoring scale reversed accordingly to indicate that the participant needs actually to read the question before responding! We notice too that participants may often defer to just circling the middle ground on a five-point rating scale. Finally, whilst the written form of questionnaires is useful because it brings about an element of anonymity, it also raises questions of literacy levels and the extent to which the written form of the question asked can really get to the nuance of human experience.

Observations

There are most certainly very qualitative approaches that can be taken to observations, for example immersing oneself in a culture and undertaking an ethnographic study in watching the world around you, but quantitative measures can also be employed in making sense of looking at things. However, in order to do this, we need to be sure we know what the thing is that we are looking at or for. If we return briefly to the chicken soup scenario, would it have been logged as dessert, chicken and sweetcorn soup or chicken soup? We might, for example, look at gender differences in aggression using observations, but beforehand we would have to create a scale of behaviours we believe constitute aggression and some sort of agreed rating of these. To some extent the PCEPS and CTS-R scales that were discussed above are an attempt to capture what we might mean by good practice in therapy. Whilst we see the discussion and disagreement on the rating scales as a useful vehicle on which to assess a trainee's development, this discussion brings with it a disadvantage to the world of quantitative research in terms of limiting the extent to which it can be considered as 'water-tight' and so allowing for it to be worked with as parametric data. In order to assess the reliability of the data obtained, researchers often double-rate the same event and look to see the extent to which their scores compare (inter-observer reliability). We might then be able to present that data collected for further statistical analysis, to see if there are any significant differences occurring between boys and girls and their levels of aggression (however we define this).

It is now to methods of data analysis that we turn.

Making sense of numbers: data analysis

It is often this part of the discussion that is the most stress-inducing for those who are rather more averse to numbers. When we introduce the dreaded statistics to our trainees, we make it clear that the intention of the session is just to outline the use of numbers and the ways that they can be of use in counselling and psychotherapy research. In terms of analysis, we always say that we will give you a flavour of what can be done and, should you want to go into further depth, we will guide you to additional resources and people. This chapter is no different. We hope that we have kept you with us so far, and in the closing sections we offer what are hopefully digestible definitions of some statistical terms that you might well come across, along with some additional reading, should you want to take your quantitative musings further.

As outlined above, the type of data that we collate drives the types of analysis that we can perform on it. If we have higher-level data (interval or ratio data to use the precise terms) then we are able to undertake statistical tests that tell us something about the significance of any relationships or patterns. We will come to this in a little while, but for now let's keep things simple.

Descriptive statistics

Let's say to begin with that you are working in a strapped-for-cash service. The service is looking to see what the average number of sessions attended is for each of its sessional therapists. Let's say that you have completed work with eight clients in this period, and the number of sessions recorded for each of them as logged in your notes is:

$$8, 7, 6, 8, 8, 6, 20, 24$$

There are three ways in which your average information could be gleaned, each of which has advantages and disadvantages. Let's initially consider the 'mean', the most commonly used measure of central tendency. The number of sessions for each of your clients would be added up and divided by the number of clients:

$$8 + 7 + 6 + 8 + 8 + 6 + 20 + 24 = 87/8 = 10.9$$

The problem of this for you is that you start to look pricey because of your outliers (those that differ greatly from the standard scores). Thus, the long-term clients that you see distort your average. You might be better using the median, where the number of sessions that each of your clients have attended is lined up and the middle value (or middle number of sessions) becomes your average. Let's see how this stacks up for you:

$$6, 6, 7, \underline{8, 8}, 8, 20, 24$$

The middle point is between the two eights, so eight becomes your average: very much better! You are (conveniently!) able to support the masking of your longer-term work by the use of the final measure of central tendency, the mode. This is the most common number of sessions that have been attended with you – excellent, eight again! Already, we begin to see how we can cook the books a little in terms of what statistics say!

Inferential statistics

Where we have the higher-level data that we referred to above, we are able to begin to make inferences about the patterns, trends, differences and relationships that occur in our data sets. You will, I am sure, have seen mention of t-tests, ANOVAs (analysis of variance), Spearman's rho and regression analyses in some of the texts to do with research and published papers. In trying to keep you with us at this point, we make it clear that further discussion of these methods of analysis are beyond the scope of this book and we refer you to follow-up texts, should you be interested in using these analyses – you can relax! However, before we close this chapter with a final activity, let's keep going for just a little bit longer with this.

If we have the type of data to be able to undertake a statistical test, then broadly speaking we are applying a recipe of data analysis to the numbers to allow us to say with a particular level of certainty that there is a real difference in the numbers collated. Let's consider another example. A questionnaire has been established to measure how brilliant you are as a therapist. Your scores out of 10 are:

$$6, 9, 4, 5, 5, 6, 5$$

Whilst you are not competitive, you are curious to know how you compare with your colleague. She has been rated:

$$6, 9, 4, 5, 5, 6, 5$$

Any significant difference? No, not at all, as the numbers are exactly the same. What about if she got:

$$6, 8, 4, 5, 5, 6, 5$$

Probably not. Only one number has changed slightly. What about:

$$5, 8, 4, 5, 5, 6, 5$$

You still don't see much difference. What about:

$$5, 8, 3, 5, 5, 6, 5$$

You don't know? The two sets of scores are looking more dissimilar, so maybe there is a significant difference here. A test may therefore be needed to check this one out. Statistical tests therefore allow us to infer with some certainty that there is a significant difference between the sets of scores and how much of this difference is due to chance or your different levels of brilliance as therapists.

We said above that to be able to undertake statistical analyses we need not only to have the level of data appropriate for such analysis, but also to have enough of it to say something of significance. Unfortunately, the tiny data sets outlined above would not be large enough to be certain of the significant difference in your levels of brilliance! However, let's just say that you were able to provide enough data and we were able to undertake an analysis of how different you were in your brilliance, you would end up with what we call a p score (with 'p' meaning probability). You might well have seen this symbol written in this way:

$$p < 0.05$$

This is a probability score which denotes how much of the difference between your sets of data are due to your differences of brilliance as therapists, or chance. Thus, the more chance that exists when looking at difference, the larger the p value becomes and the less significant the difference. This results in lower confidence of there being a 'real' or 'significant' difference between the two of you. Broadly speaking, in order to say that there is a significant difference between the two of you, we look for a probability level of less than 5 per cent chance explaining the differences in your scores; this is expressed as $p < 0.05$. The greater the differences in your scores of brilliance, the less that chance factors will play a role in explaining the difference. We might, for example, if the scores are very different, end up with a p value of $p < 0.001$ or even less. This indicates that less than 0.001 per cent of the difference between you both is due to chance, or more optimistically for you that 99.9 per cent of the difference is due to your pure brilliance as a therapist! Great for you to feed back to your line manager, though not so great for your colleague.

The papers by Coolican listed at the end of this chapter are helpful as follow-up reading to the brief introduction offered above.

ACTIVITY 12: Is this book helping?

You probably need a pause after this, and so at this point in the book we ask you to consider how useful you are finding its contents. In particular we return to the second activity we asked you to engage in during the introduction chapter. This activity asked you to identify the goals that you have whilst you are reading this book, and we introduced our specially devised SARA questionnaire. These two activities hope to encourage you to consider how well the book is meeting your needs by reflecting upon your earlier scores as a point of comparison.

This activity attempts to:

1   provide examples of different types of quantitative research data
2   encourage the reader to reflect upon the usage of goal-based outcome measures

and

3   provide a reflection of how individuals' awareness of research topics may be changing as they engage with the contents of the book.

The activity

As mentioned above, this activity revisits the tasks that we first asked you to complete in the Introduction chapter of this book. These asked you to reflect upon your goals for the book and to rate your knowledge in specific areas. In much the same way that we can use questionnaires to measure progress in therapy, we can use the goal questions and SARA to consider how your understanding of research topics might be developing. In doing so, we ask you to do two things: 1) to rate the attainment of the goals you identified at the outset of this book on a scale of 1 to 5 (1 reflecting that the goal has not been attained and 5 that it has been completely attained); 2) to complete the SARA questionnaire once again. In the latter instance, the earlier measures can therefore act as a yardstick to consider how things may have changed. Activity Box 12 outlines the activity once again.

ACTIVITY BOX 12

Is this book helping?

Please undertake the two tasks outlined below.

What are your goals?

Reflect upon the goals that you identified at the outset of this text (noted in the Introduction). Rate each of these goals using a scale of 1–5 (1 = the goal has not been attained, 5 = the goal has been fully attained).

　　NB: You may want to identify further goals for continuing to read the book at this stage. Also, if you are just dipping into this chapter you may want to identify new goals for reading this text and rate them.

How research literate are you?

The SARA questionnaire

Please rate your knowledge of each topic noted below on a scale of 0–5 (0 = I know nothing about this, 5 = I am very aware of this issue).

- The research that underpins therapy
- What is the purpose of research?
- The issues related to preparing to undertake research
- The impact that research has upon the researcher
- Quantitative research
- Qualitative research
- The ethical issues within therapy research
- The arenas in which counselling and psychotherapy research is talked about

---

Your findings

At this point, we hold our breath and hope that your engagement with the text is positive. In some ways we know that a positive score is likely, as, by getting through to Chapter 6 of the book, we can make the assumption that you were not automatically put off by the style of the text (a potential bias in our sample).

More specifically it will be interesting to reflect upon how well this book is meeting your goals and whether you can see it helping to improve your awareness of research issues. In relation to the former, your answers are likely to be so idiosyncratic that it proves difficult for us to pre-empt them here. You may, however, find that as you read the text your goals have shifted, developed or been met. In relation to the latter task we would anticipate that you should notice that the earlier topics have shown more improvement than the latter ones (if you have read the text in chronological chapter order, that is). Thus, our question at this stage is, 'Is this the case?'

Our findings

This section briefly summarises fictional SARA scores for an individual reading this book. Table 3 provides a summary of this data. Graphs 4 and 5 also summarise the scores, with Graph 4 providing a summary of the individual questions and Graph 5 providing a summary of the mean score of all components of the questionnaire.

If we consider the summary of total scores (visually represented in Graph 5) we can see that for this individual there has been relatively little development in their understanding of research. The scores move from 3.125 to 3.375. In contrast, if we take the individual variables for SARA we can see that some areas have seen a great deal of movement; for example, Series 1 (which relates to the importance that research has for therapists) has increased by four points and Series 3 (which relates to the issues related

Table 3 A summary of the SARA data

Question	Pre-score	Mid-score
1	1	5
2	3	3
3	5	3
4	0	2
5	5	5
6	2	2
7	5	5
8	4	2
Mean	3.125	3.375

Graph 4   A summary of individual SARA scores at two intervals

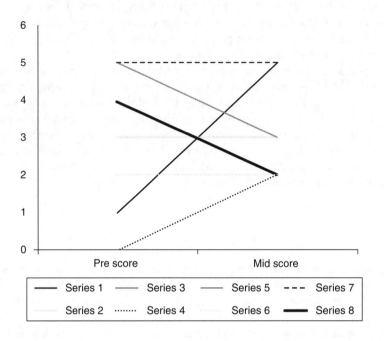

Graph 5   A summary of cumulative SARA scores at two intervals

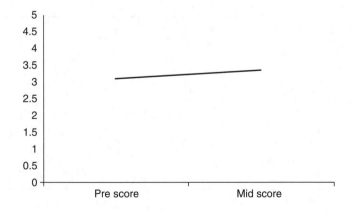

to being prepared to undertake research) has seen a negative impact upon the scores (reducing by two points). We could reflect upon each of these variables in turn, but this is enough for our discussion points for the time being.

Discussion

In reflecting upon the findings noted above, we could conclude that the book has had relatively little impact upon our fictional person. We would however have to be a little cautious in these conclusions due to the messiness of the data that has been collected. For instance, the respondent may have just ticked the boxes randomly to get rid of the questionnaire-wielding researcher. Alternatively the scores might reflect some of the complexities in human processes. For instance, if we consider Series 3 in which things appear to have worsened around the individual's preparedness to undertake research, we might actually see this as a normal process. For example, the respondent may have read the chapter and realised that they didn't know as much about research as they initially felt they did, and thus they find themselves recalibrating themselves. Such a process should not be treated lightly and has been reported within the therapy literature, with individuals noting that they get worse before getting better. Also, if we consider Series 1 in which most improvement is noted, how do we know that this is due to the contents of the book? At this point we direct you in two directions: 1) back to the earlier section of this chapter discussing the stories in numbers; 2) forwards towards discussions of mixing research methods. The former reminds the reader of some of the politics in quantitative research design, while the latter reflects upon how quantitative and qualitative research methods can sit well side by side.

Mixing methods

Quantitative research is incredibly influential within the world of therapy. As indicated in this and earlier chapters, the findings of this type of research often have great sway in the commissioning of services and provide compelling headlines to summarise how well therapeutic services work. What are often ignored in these discussions are the assumptions that are made when creating and interpreting findings. For instance, 'What decisions led to the choice of particular questions being included in standardised questionnaires?' or, 'How might a respondent be interpreting the questions that they're answering?' Research into psychological phenomena is without doubt a complex endeavour and often we need to think beyond the headlines for satisfactory answers. One way of doing this is by mixing quantitative data with qualitative data, an approach that is often called mixed methods research. Such an approach aims to make best use of the advantages of both types of data, with qualitative data being used to 'add meaning' to quantitative results, and quantitative data used to 'add precision' to qualitative findings (Johnson and Onwuegbuzie, 2004: 21).

This is exemplified practically and summed up in Goss and Mearns' (1997b) work evaluating employee counselling services:

> Relying solely on change to numerical data would fail to communicate the vital importance of the service in human terms. Equally, stories of therapy cannot tell us the clearly quantifiable value of the service. (1997b: 341)

Thus, in utilising both quantitative and qualitative data, research projects can therefore produce richer data sets and enable authors to provide fuller pictures of the phenomena being examined.

Within the world of counselling and psychotherapy direct attention to mixing methods has proven relatively limited. Traditionally individuals have been firmly encamped within specific conceptual frameworks of research, the natural scientists utilising experimental designs within one corner and the social scientists with a more qualitative bias in the other (Goss and Mearns, 1997a). Mixed methods researchers are often more pragmatic in their views of research and aim to use what gets the job done (see Morgan, 2007, for a philosophical discussion of such research). It is thus with the intent of seeing beyond the warring of research paradigms, alongside the hope of retaining a focus upon the stakeholders of the studies rather than a concentration upon ivory tower-based paradigmatic debate, that has led to the call for more accepting pluralistic stances towards research. In practice this has begun to manifest itself in the completion of studies that use a combination of methods either broadly (e.g. Hanley, 2009) or as a part of an advocated protocol, such as those advocated in systematic case studies (see McLeod, 2010).

At this point we stop, before creating a whole chapter about mixed methods. For the interested reader we do however encourage further reading in this area to get your teeth fully into the nuances of such work.

The student voice: Aaron Sefi

As a counsellor, researcher and now service manager, I have fallen in and out of love with statistics (and the ways that they are applied) many times since first being introduced to the world of quantitative research in counselling. Even though I now have learned to love numbers (driven by a pragmatic belief in their necessity), the first time I opened the 'green book' that regularly came with my membership of the BACP (their research journal *Counselling and Psychotherapy Research*), I was initially overwhelmed, and perhaps repelled. But then I found what this chapter refers to as the 'headlines' and then I was hooked! We make stories with research, and then they get treated as truth – how very interesting!

Sometimes I feel that counselling is irreducible to figures and graphs, and yet I recognise the need to evaluate what we are doing in some form that is translatable and comparable to other forms of help. In that, the drive is to 'legitimise' counselling, and hold it up for professional scrutiny. This chapter picks up on the fact that statistical findings play a significant role in the minds of policy-makers and government agendas, and this is increasingly trickling down into evidence-based commissioning. And this state of affairs is what drives many counsellors' reluctant acceptance of statistical findings – seen as a necessary evil reflecting the attitudes of the day, which somehow don't fit with the ideals of (predominantly) humanistic counselling.

I think this fear-driven mentality limits so much possibility, not least because there is an argument that counsellor engagement with the measures (that lead to these statistical findings) could actually show better outcomes. And the principle of what works for whom – and when and why and how it works – needs to be at the heart of any motive for intervention, if you want to justify your intervention to the outside world.

So statistical findings sit a bit like oil in the calm waters of professional practice. But how calm are these waters really? As discussed in this book, we are in an inquisitive profession, asking questions – doing research is what we do all the time.

My experiences of using questionnaires such as the YP-CORE (see Twigg et al., 2009) in routine evaluation have raised many important issues for me. The questionnaire, and many like it, can show in a clear and simple way whether counselling might have an impact upon a client's level of wellbeing or distress. If our main aim in doing research is to raise the profile of counselling within the wider world, then the use of psychometrics in the *laboratory style* of an RCT is essential to tell a convincing story (in the present climate).

My foray into the world of practitioner-researcher has been a unique challenge. I have developed an inkling of practice wisdom through my work with young people, and this does not always match up to the results produced in routine evaluation. It raises important questions around subjectivity, and what value an objective measure can possibly have beyond that of indirectly paying my bills.

I suspect that many counsellors are averse to statistics because in some way they represent the prevailing cultural values of scientific positivism (the belief that there is one truth) that arguably become more powerful in times of scarce resources (such as an economic downturn). I think this comes down mainly to the way that statistics are used. Using them to define a truth flies in the face of humanistic counselling and its intrinsic allowance of a multitude of truths or possibilities. With the trend towards determining therapeutic 'competencies' as outlined here, it is seemingly inevitable that all counselling will become *measurable* to some degree. Whilst no counsellor worth their salt would deny the need for feedback loops, the anxiety of being measured against something or someone else, and how that is used to justify funding, is surely at the heart of a lot of resistance to statistics.

This chapter introduces the notion of mixing methods in research, and this is for me at the heart of good counselling research – allowing for the need for headlines, and hoping that some people will scan a bit further down to read the back-story. Most counsellors I know are not interested in *whether* counselling works. They know it does (or at least they think they know). But they tend to be more interested in how, why, and under which circumstances. The development of goal-based outcome measures allows for this interplay of statistics with qualitative 'stories' of counselling, as do the systematic case studies (McLeod, 2010) as mentioned in this chapter. These also perhaps soften the hard edges of statistics. The danger in mixed methods is to have a particular emphasis on one side (i.e. numbers) and just tack on the other (i.e. narrative). Both need to play an important and interrelated role to offer meaning to the other. Only in this way can the water of 'practice-wisdom' and the oil of statistical findings mix to make beautiful patterns!

Summary points

- Quantitative research can often be viewed with fear by counsellors and psychotherapists; however, studies of this kind can potentially have a significant political impact.
- Quantitative data can provide a convenient means of consulting with large numbers of people in an energy-efficient way.
- Quantitative approaches require a pinning-down or measuring of variables which might well present some difficulties in the work of counselling and therapy.
- Quantitative analysis provides a recipe for what to do with research data, which can be attractive. The requirements for whether these 'recipes' can be applied is dependent on a number of factors, for example, the level of data collected (nominal, ordinal, interval or ratio) and the design of the study.
- Whilst there are complex mechanisms that exist to make sense of statistical data, there are numerous simpler methods for making sense of the data that you routinely generate in your practice.
- Mixed methods research designs combine quantitative and qualitative research methods. This approach can be a very useful way of getting the most out of the different types of data.

FURTHER READING

For the next step on the journey to quantitative research you might want to read John McLeod's chapter 'Using quantitative methods' in order to focus upon the topic. Additionally, Part 1 of Ladislav Timulak's book also provides a useful overview of how quantitative research has been used in counselling and psychotherapy research. The references are noted below:

McLeod, J. (2003) *Doing Counselling Research*, Second Edition. London: Sage.
Timulak, L. (2008) *Research in Psychotherapy and Counselling*. London: Sage.

A very helpful introduction to some key quantitative terms from a therapeutic perspective is given in the following journal articles:

Dyer, C., Joseph, S. and Coolican, H. (2005) 'Dealing with paired datasets: graphical and statistical approaches', *Counselling and Psychotherapy Research,* 5 (4): 256–7.
Joseph, S., Dyer, C. and Coolican, H. (2005) 'What does p < .05 mean?', *Counselling and Psychotherapy Research,* 5 (2): 105–6.
Joseph, S., Dyer, C. and Coolican, H. (2005) 'Means and standard deviations explained', *Counselling and Psychotherapy Research,* 5 (3): 256–7.

A research methods text that is presented in a very reader-friendly way is Andy Field's *Discovering Statistics*. This is a large text and it covers a wide range of topics (probably everything you're possibly going to need). There are a few great anecdotes in it too.

Field, A. (2013) *Discovering Statistics Using SPSS*, Fourth Edition. London: Sage.

Finally, we would also outline the developing body of literature around mixed methods research. As a starting point try:

Creswell, J. and Plano-Clark, V. (2010) *Designing and Conducting Mixed Methods Research*, Second Edition. London: Sage.

7

Qualitative Research: Collecting and Making Sense of Talk, Thoughts and Feelings in Therapy Research

Abstract

In this chapter we consider qualitative approaches to research. These approaches are initially described before introducing some of the common rationales for adopting such a stance. In particular we focus upon the collection of rich information such as the words, thoughts and feelings of individuals. As with other chapters we describe the activities that we (as trainers) have found useful when working with students and provide common responses/ reflections from our students themselves. Following this, we embed these thoughts into the broader literature about qualitative research, introduce some examples of where work of this kind has impacted upon practice, and reflect upon what makes a good piece of qualitative research. Matt Shorrock, an experienced psychotherapist and one of our existing trainees undertaking a qualitative research project, then has his say on the matter. Finally, further reading is suggested for those contemplating following up the subject matter further – maybe even conducting a piece of qualitative research themselves.

THOUGHT BOX 7

How do your clients rate you?

If you asked the clients that you work with how valuable they found their meetings with you:

- What kind of answers would you anticipate? (Long or short, detailed or brief, etc.)
- How would you be able to make sense of their words? (Would their comments resonate with those of other clients? Can you identify common themes?)
- How TRUE would their words be? And what may have influenced their responses?

What is qualitative enquiry?

Research is often stereotyped as a stuffy process in which people in white coats (most likely with a clipboard in hand) collect an abundance of information that then needs to be thoroughly number crunched. Although, in some instances, this does resonate with some approaches to research, the qualitative researcher aims to explore the worlds that individuals inhabit and make sense of the stories that individuals tell them. Thus, in adopting this approach, it is more likely that the researcher would engage another person in some sort of conversation to gain a sense of how they experience a particular phenomenon. Some definitions of qualitative research include the following:

> The primary aim of qualitative research is to develop an understanding of how the social world is constructed. (McLeod, 2011: 3)

> Language-based research, in which experiences, perceptions, observations, etc. are not reduced to numerical form. (Cooper, 2008: 186)

As should be implicit in these descriptions, numerous ways of gathering qualitative data can be adopted. Furthermore, it is very apparent that it can be helpfully understood by what it is not, notably a means to reducing text or observations to numbers.

Now consider the questions raised in Thought Box 7. It wouldn't be out of the ordinary to expect clients to provide detailed responses to such an open question. These may be multi-faceted and include positive and negative elements. For instance, in my own therapy with a person-centred counsellor I (TH) remember valuing the warmth within the meetings, but I also got frustrated by the lack of input from the counsellor at times. Such a simplistic observation of these differing types of comment may make the beginnings of a useful thematic analysis about client observations of the person-centred approach. However, in thinking about how I would answer the third question posed ('How TRUE would *my* words be? And what may have influenced *my* responses?') I would have to hold my hands up and admit my response would vary greatly depending upon how I was asked. On ending this relationship I think I probably said to the counsellor something like, 'Thanks ... I found our meetings very helpful' and did not mention my frustration at any point during this conversation. However, if I was given the opportunity to discuss our work with a neutral third party, or requested information once our meeting had ended, I may have been more forthcoming. Therefore, in this case I presented an element of the full picture to the counsellor, but there was still more to reveal (an outcome that has also been observed more systematically in the research literature, see Rennie, 1994). Although it will never be possible for a qualitative researcher to gain a full picture of any phenomenon, it is their responsibility to capture an essence of it as best they can. Additionally, having a sense of the elements of the phenomenon that have not been captured, and the reasons for this omission, is incredibly important. It is with these complexities in mind that we approach this chapter.

In the following sections we aim to provide an overview of common processes whilst undertaking a piece of qualitative research. In doing so we introduce how individuals perceive such work, how they go about conducting such a project, and what they do with the data when they get it. Each of these sections is then briefly discussed in relation to the existing literature about this topic.

Considerations regarding qualitative enquiry

A qualitative mode of enquiry is often the preferred route for students researching counselling and the psychological therapies. Unfortunately this is not only because it fits their topic better but also because they might have a strong aversion for numbers! On an epistemological basis this is not good enough and counsellors need to be well versed in multiple approaches of research to make sense of the vast array of research findings that are relevant to their practice. Research designs therefore need to be constructed in an informed manner and be led by the topic rather than fear and avoidance. However, even if a qualitative study is adopted, there are major considerations to be taken into account. The activity we come to now attempts to get students to focus upon potential complexities.

ACTIVITY 13: Qualitative research – What could go wrong?

Once individuals have been introduced to what qualitative research is, there is often a visible sense of relief – one that may be verbalised as 'Phew!!! I thought research was all about complicated numbers.' The emphasis on examining a phenomenon in some depth therefore appears very attractive to many students on this surface level. To account for this it has been useful to stop, remove any rose-tinted spectacles that may have been donned, and reflect upon the potential negative side of such work. This activity aims to do this head-on in a simple reflective exercise.

This activity attempts to:

1   encourage the reader to reflect upon their initial perceptions about qualitative research
2   support the reader in considering the strengths and weaknesses of qualitative research

and

3   help the reader to reflect upon the place qualitative research has when commissioning bodies decide upon what services to fund (note the similarity to the aim of Activity 3 in Chapter 2).

The activity

Based upon the brief introduction to qualitative research, we ask you to enter into a dialogue with yourself about the nature of this approach to research (alternatively you could work with a willing colleague if one is available). If you can, imagine interviewing yourself for about 30 minutes. Draft yourself some questions (an interview schedule) and imagine how you might go about probing deeper to get a good sense of how you really feel about the topic – this is where counselling skills can come in very handy. Feel free to take this wherever you want and see where you end up (Activity Box 13 provides an overview of the activity and some questions to start you off if needed).

ACTIVITY BOX 13

Qualitative research: what could go wrong?

Reflect upon your views about qualitative research.
Consider the following questions:

- Why might qualitative research be useful?
- What areas of concern do you have about taking a qualitative approach to your research? (E.g. Data generation? Data analysis? Ethics?)
- How might others perceive qualitative research?

Your findings

On reflecting upon the task it would be interesting to hear about your thoughts and feelings about such work. Did you share the sentiment of relief described earlier when we noted that research was not all about complicated statistics? Or did the idea of qualitative research remind you of poor science? In fact, maybe you felt a bit of both –

'Yes I do like the idea that research is more than just coming up with a number (for instance, can Douglas Adams' [1979] answer "42" ever truly sum up the meaning of life?). However I don't think the view of a small group of people can ever really be very useful. For instance, isn't this type of work just anecdotal storytelling really?'

If this is the type of dialogue you had with yourself then this would reflect something that echoes the conversations within the classes we run.

Our findings

As indicated above, we would commonly ask our trainees to undertake a similar activity in pairs – one taking on the role of interviewer and the other as interviewee (thus practising a qualitative data collection technique in process). To outline some of the issues that students raise we have summarised the comments we received within one large group feedback session below. These points might sound a little familiar.

1 To what extent can our voice be aired in qualitative research? And how can this be done in an appropriate and balanced way so as not to result in a narcissistic piece of work with associated methodological flaws?
2 How do we attend to issues of reliability and validity, and ensure that the work is as 'watertight' as possible and can stand up to rigorous challenge?

3   How can we speak to other audiences with confidence and communicate messages from the work when perhaps it has been based on something quite unique and a small data set?

4   How do we ensure that all data is captured in the analysis and we do not just attend to that which fits into our pre-set research questions?

5   How do we ensure that the codings and categories that emerge do justice to the data collected and echo the subtleties of what the participants were sharing? Specifically, how can we be sure that we don't just take a reductionist position in dealing with the data and keep it neat and tidy so that we achieve our qualification?

6   How do we decide what the data is? For example, how is silence used in interviews? Or, how is material regarding the dynamics between people in a focus group used?

7   Are qualitative findings really any use at all?

Discussion

Many of the points discussed above deal with issues of reliability and validity: concepts that are central to quantitative work and perhaps more easily established in a number-based piece of research with regard to sample size, significance levels or inter-observer reliability coefficients. These points are viewed slightly differently in qualitative research but, it could be argued, are even more important to qualitative analysis. For instance, qualitative approaches often have a reputation for being softer and more subjective and, with this in mind, it is important for procedures of data analysis to be fully described and justified. Likewise any conclusions reached need to be transparent and clearly articulated for the reader to make up their mind about the strength of argument posed (thus the issue of trustworthiness is often considered rather than reliability).

In terms of the validity of the conclusions that are drawn from the data, qualitative studies often acknowledge that a multitude of interpretations could be presented as the 'truth' (or most useful understanding of the data). In accounting for this, validity in qualitative research therefore refers to the extent to which the presentation represents a trustworthy account of the data that has been collected. Methods therefore need to be fully outlined in relation to how the data has been analysed and thus allow other researchers to check the consistency of findings (inter-observer reliability). It is also important that we attend to negative or deviant cases (i.e. those that don't fit in with the question set or majority views held) and that the data is used systematically to explain to the reader how the conclusions relate to the data.

In furthering ideas of validity and trustworthiness, it is commonly viewed as good practice to report findings back to participants in the study to check the respondents' validation of findings reached. This can help to check the credibility of the findings (e.g. Elliott, Fischer and Rennie, 1999) but is not always viewed as commensurate with the purpose and philosophy of some research methods (e.g. see Smith, Flowers and Larkin, 2009). Additionally, the transparency of the qualitative researcher can be tracked by reflecting on their own experiences of undertaking the research, their role as researcher and the impact that this might have on the study and the findings reached. This adds a distinct strength to a qualitative study in that the researcher's role and impact is made overt and transparent in a way that is often dismissed in quantitative studies; although their impact is just as central it might be camouflaged as experimenter effects and thought about less thoroughly (Lennie and West, 2010). Clearly, in the final write-up, decisions need to be made about how these reflections are presented in the final report with regard to writing in the third or first person, inclusion of the reflections as data, and structuring of the piece. Often resolution of these dilemmas causes concern to students as they anticipate the 'fit' that their final piece might have with the demands of the awarding institution and if the work fits neatly enough to be understood within the 'research ethos' of the department. This is a particular concern for Doctorate students when contemplating who is being invited to examine their thesis.

Qualitative research: a rationale

At this juncture we consider the rationale behind using qualitative approaches of research. As we have touched upon above it is by no means an easy option, and conducting good-quality qualitative research can be incredibly difficult. Additionally, the political impact of qualitative research often proves much less than quantitative research. So why head down this challenging and potentially unrewarding pathway? The simple answer is that there is often no other way to help us understand the intricacies of our therapeutic practice. As we noted earlier, McLeod (2011: 3) states that:

> The primary aim of qualitative research is to develop an understanding of how the social world is constructed.

Qualitative methods of gathering data offer rich pickings and can be used to make sense of the often complex phenomena that we are interested in. They often rely upon the actual words of those involved and provide detailed overviews of how they have made sense of events in their lives. For example, in our own work we have utilised qualitative approaches to look at the inner workings of the therapeutic relationship in online counselling (Hanley, 2009, 2012), to understand spiritual dimensions of therapy (West, 1997, 1998, 2009) and to explore counselling trainees' experiences of attending personal development groups (Lennie, 2007). The flexibility of such designs proves a major strength, particularly as we have only scratched the surface of what we understand about human relations in general, let alone in specific therapeutic contexts.

Linked to the potential to learn more about a wide variety of specific topics, qualitative approaches also enable research to be undertaken with hard-to-reach groups, or groups of limited numbers. In contrast to the previous chapter, which looks at collecting quantitative data that may be generalised to wider populations, qualitative research acknowledges that certain groups will be a challenge to contact and that although respondents are limited, data can be rich. Thus, feedback from small numbers of individuals can enable researchers to gather information about peoples' experiences that may not otherwise get heard, for instance, when exploring the views of homeless people (Cormack, 2009), women who self-harm (Walker, 2009) and gay men's experience of counselling (Mair, 2003).

In contemplating when it is appropriate to utilise such an approach it is necessary to consider the questions that are being posed. If you are hoping to compare a client's rating of distress at the start of counselling with that at the end, clearly a quantitative approach would prove most appropriate. In contrast, if you hope to understand the processes that led to changes within therapy, then a qualitative approach would most likely provide the best results. Essentially, research questions are at the core of any research project and they provide an insight into the design that might be utilised. They hold the project together in terms of what you choose to put in the literature, the methods that you adopt and how you present and make sense of the findings. It could be said that the research question is like the word 'Blackpool' that runs through a piece of Blackpool rock – it should hold your dissertation together. Therefore, decisions to adopt an approach need to meet the needs of the questions posed, not the needs of the person doing the research. Thus, unfortunately for some, qualitative research does not prove an appropriate rationale for avoiding quantitative methods for those who do not like statistics.

Finally, an issue that must not be underplayed in any qualitative research is the place that ethics have in our work. Just as a counsellor, psychotherapist or counselling psychologist works within a code of ethics (e.g. BACP, 2010; BPS, 2009) such documents also underpin the world of research. Gone are the days where researchers can coax individuals to take part in projects, and it is imperative that researchers work with the participant's wellbeing in mind. Commonly, general ethical documents are complemented by organisational statements about research (e.g. Bond, 2004; BPS, 2010). These provide more specific guidance and advice about such work and often note that individuals should be able to give informed consent to take part in research, be free to opt out at any stage and, when desired, not be identifiable in any write-ups of the work. At the heart of these decisions is respect for the individual giving up their time to support your project. These points are further considered in Chapter 8.

Collecting talk, thoughts and feelings: data generation

Previous chapters have already highlighted the strong position that the counsellor is in when entering the world of research. Much of this section is therefore about encouraging practitioners to utilise these skills in a research setting, reframing their skills as 'research' rather than 'therapy' and adjusting to related ethical and methodological implications of this shift. For example, if a counsellor has the skills to facilitate a deepening insight within the client, often beyond their initial expectation of what they might say, then the counsellor researcher also has the skill to access data that goes beyond the participant's expectation of the interview exercise. This then has implications in relation to the extent to which participants are able give their informed consent to the study. With this in mind, consent potentially becomes more of a process that needs to be checked throughout. People in interviews will often find themselves revealing more than they intended to. It is the sign of a good interviewer and such skills need to be used carefully, appropriately and respectfully.

Equally the researcher will have to make decisions in relation to the extent to which the research conversation remains focused on the question set. In therapy, a conversation might freely move across a multitude of topics. If research is based around one topic, decisions may therefore need to be made regarding the possibility of research conversations going off at a tangent and whether any interconnections between the data and their meanings might also constitute data. Additionally the counsellor researcher is attuned to understanding body language, silences and voice intonations and will have to make decisions in relation to the extent to which they are counted in some way as data.

Another area that can add a further layer to proceedings is the research method adopted. For example, talk can be collected individually or in groups. One-to-one interviews might be a more familiar forum for counsellors, but the skills counsellors and psychotherapists have can also be transferred to a focus group setting. This leap proves to be the focus of our next activity.

ACTIVITY 14: What do your colleagues really think about ...?

As has been mentioned in earlier chapters, a major part of our teaching relies upon students learning through doing. Within class, this activity provides a perfect example of this type of teaching as we invite students actively to develop and conduct a focus group of their own. Such a live demonstration of this method of collecting data helps to bring it to life and provides an enormous amount of fodder for discussion. It also has the benefit of offering some students the opportunity to practise skills in hosting a group and others the opportunity to experience what it might feel like from the perspective of a group member.

As will be evident, we cannot get you to go through the whole class activity, but we can encourage you along a similar path by planning a focus group and considering the method's strengths and weaknesses.

This activity attempts to:

1 encourage the reader actively to begin to develop a qualitative research question
2 get the reader to design a focus group interview schedule

and

3 highlight some of the strengths and weaknesses of qualitative research methods of collecting data.

The activity

When trainees are contemplating what topics to research, we often begin by asking them what it is that they are curious about. This activity begins by inviting you to undertake a similar process and explore your curious side. What do you want to know about your colleagues? (Or what might prove a little interesting to know more about?)

This could be anything, and for the purposes of this exercise needn't be about counselling. When given this scope in small groups, one of our classes came up with two counselling-related questions. These were 1) whether personal therapy should be mandatory for counselling trainees, and 2) how recent graduates of counsellor training make sense of therapeutic integration. These topics were refined into the following simple questions:

RQ1: Should personal therapy be mandatory for trainee counsellors?

RQ2: What does 'integration' mean to counsellors on completion of an integrative training programme?

These groups will be discussed further in a little while, but for the time being, do you have a topic? And can you phrase it as a simple question similar to the ones above? If yes, then your next task is to think up four or five related sub-questions that would help you find out more about the topic. ('Why might personal therapy be inappropriate?' or 'What might be lost from training if individuals do not experience personal therapy?') If you are struggling to find a topic, then maybe contemplate what questions you might ask about one of the questions our students came up with.

To end, once you have come up with your list of questions (which you could once again call your interview schedule) we ask you to contemplate how you imagine the answers to your questions might differ if you asked them in a one-to-one interview. See Activity Box 14 for a summary of what we're asking.

ACTIVITY BOX 14

What do your colleagues really think about …?

Task 1: Create a research question about your topic of interest.

Task 2: Create a list of 4 or 5 questions related to this question.

  Finally

Task 3: How might the data that you generate differ if you asked these questions in a one-to-one interview rather than a focus group?

Your findings

So, how did you get on? Did you actually manage to come up with something that interests you? And was it related to counselling? As should be evident from earlier sections of this book, there are so many questions to ask about therapeutic practice that we hope you found something. You might want to return to Chapter 5 to consider whether your research idea is meaningful or not, but for now that's a separate issue.

A more challenging side to the task might have been to phrase your interest as a simple question. Often people get a little tangled up in attempting to create questions that are potentially too sophisticated – sometimes less can be more and there is no need to over-complicate things. Additionally, being specific can be very helpful. Does you question outline the topic of interest, the group under scrutiny and the setting? For instance, you may want to explore the therapeutic alliance within school-based counselling with young people. But then there is also the question of what you wish to do with this information. In the above situation you might therefore ask:

- How do young people *rate* the therapeutic alliance in school-based counselling?

or

- How do young people *experience* the therapeutic alliance in school-based counselling?

Such minor changes make a large difference in the focus of the study and also the research methods adopted. In the above case you might anticipate the first question being answered with quantitative methods as it looks at rating people, whilst the second question wants to understand the experience of the young people and is thus more likely to be qualitative. What was the focus of your question?

Once you have a question you can then consider the questions that you would ask in a focus group setting. Counsellors are often quite adept at creating such questions owing to their existing awareness of the subject matter. We'll therefore leave you to ponder whether they would have provided rich data here.

The final issue to consider is that of the nature of the focus group data. Did you get the sense that you would get different information if you asked your questions in a one-to-one setting? Some topics might work well in a group, whilst others might not go anywhere. In particular, if you were interested in a sensitive topic such as sexual abuse, you might have the sense that hosting a focus group might inhibit participants from sharing their stories. Alternatively, looking at counsellors' experiences of completing paperwork might benefit from the dynamics of group interactions. All these types of issues prove important in successfully completing a rich qualitative research project.

Our findings

Within this section I feel like we are about to disappoint you. We have sown the seed of some interesting questions about counselling and psychotherapy training but we are not going to discuss explicitly the data that was collected. You may therefore feel inspired to follow up the topics in the research literature, within which there is much discussion related to both of these issues – in relation to the latter question, you will even find one paper which was the culmination of the student's Master's research project (Lowndes and Hanley, 2010). However, that aside, our interests here are methodological. How did the facilitators find hosting their focus groups? Brief statements from each of the group facilitators are presented in turn below (these are summaries from verbal feedback within the class group – please note that they are not verbatim quotes although they have been presented in this format).

RQ1: Should personal therapy be mandatory for trainee counsellors?

'I tried to be inclusive and get everyone's opinion. This led to some people feeling that they were being rushed into giving an answer before they had really thought things through. It may have been wiser as facilitator not to have given my opinion on the question posed as this may have shut people down and stopped them thinking about their stance rather than opening up new possibilities.

It emerged that there was an overwhelming majority favouring one outcome. However, one member took the polar opposite view to the rest of the group. This led to conflict between them and another group member. My understanding at this stage, based primarily on bodily signals, was that this participant felt slightly under attack from the rest of the group. I felt the need to intervene and acknowledge that each participant had the right to their own opinion however much the rest of the group may disagree.

Additionally, my instinct was that this participant took such a strong view against the majority, not just because he believed in it but also as a stance against my directive style of running the group. So, I think that in some way he acted as a spokesperson for the rest of the group at an emotional level, i.e. they were angry at being "forced" to give an answer.'

RQ2: What does 'integration' mean to counsellors on completion of an integrative training programme?

'My main reflection of this group was the important role that curiosity as a research skill played in the activity. In particular ensuring that this was demonstrated and conveyed to the participants seemed vital. With this in mind, I felt the need to offer something akin to person-centred ground rules and remain open and be accepting of the views that might be expressed.

There were sampling issues that impacted on this group. The research question related to what counsellors make of integration post qualification. Due to the nature of the training group one individual had come from a different training route to everyone else. So that this person was not alienated from the group, I, as facilitator, responded by saying that I was still very interested to hear what the individual might have to say. It was interesting to note that this had not been heard by the participant within the debriefing part of the session.'

Discussion

As a first point of discussion, it is always noteworthy how valuable counselling skills are to those entering into the realms of qualitative research interviewing. In the above examples, both facilitators are beginning to enter into sophisticated discussions about their role within the group and their influence upon it. Not backing away from such discussions and being mindful of the roles we play in research prove an essential part of good research of this kind.

Some of the complexities associated with the dynamics of group interviews come through in these brief reflections. Much as group therapy requires different skills to one-to-one therapy, so do focus groups when contrasted with individual interviews. In these instances, the facilitator often took the role of a curious observer or a devil's advocate in providing a springboard for participants to share views that deviated from the emerging norm of the group. There was a particular emphasis on some of the dilemmas associated with collecting differing opinions within focus groups, particularly as a consensus view can often result from collecting data in this way.

Ethical issues were reconsidered after the groups had ended. In particular, the question of how research activities may impact upon individuals was considered. As researchers there is a responsibility to do no harm to individuals, and discussing issues related to counselling, whether one-to-one or in a group, may churn up difficult thoughts or feelings in participants. Additionally for us as tutors, this added an ethical dimension in the way that we deliver research training. In attempting to take a more experiential approach to teaching research and getting students to act as participants/researchers who are using different research techniques, we are potentially exposing students to experiences that might trigger some difficult feelings – for example, an individual may have minority views in a group situation. Thus, care needs to be taken when entering into this arena. However, we believe that such activities are appropriate and congruent within the area under consideration (i.e. counselling and psychotherapy), and furthermore it is desirable that research training in counselling should have a personal development aspect to it.

Collecting talk, thoughts and feelings continued

There are numerous ways that counsellors can collect qualitative data. These are often described as the 'methods' that are adopted by researchers. As has been noted, counsellors commonly utilise approaches such as one-to-one interviews, focus groups or questionnaires that look for detailed responses. Additionally, counsellors' reflexive journals; and creative work based upon their practice may also go into the mix. Some practitioners may also conduct observations of therapy in practice (usually through recordings) or systematic reviews of existing databases of literature to come to qualitative conclusions; however, in our experience these are much less common than other approaches. Thus, qualitative researchers are often encouraged to be creative and use methods that collect the best data for the task at hand.

Most frequently students on our courses undertake some sort of interview with those taking part in their research projects. These include those that are unstructured in nature, semi-structured and structured. Each of these styles can vary, depending upon the research questions that have been posed. An exploratory study may therefore utilise an unstructured approach so as to support the participant/co-researcher in telling their story, while a structured interview may be keen to keep participants harnessed to a particular topic of interest. Predominantly a middle ground is sought through semi-structured interviews, with students seeking to explore the phenomenon of interest but not stray too far away from it. One of the major strengths of the one-to-one interview for the world of counselling and psychotherapy is its privacy. In many instances, particularly when interviewing people who are, or have been, in therapy, it proves more appropriate to provide the interviewee with a secure setting akin to that provided to a client in therapy. Such an environment can help to facilitate the generation of rich data on a wide range of intimate subject matters.

Group interviews or focus groups can follow comparable paths to interviews, with unstructured, semi-structured or structured activities being undertaken. The major difference here is that the interaction between participants can prove invaluable. It can spark discussions that would not occur in one-to-one interviews and their energy can, at times, prove contagious – thus generating data of a unique quality. Researchers can therefore engineer groups to contain people with similar/different beliefs with the hope of observing the dialogues that emerge. In doing so, as when working therapeutically with groups, great care needs to be taken when considering the topics to be discussed and those involved – focus groups should not end up being like a daytime talk show! Inevitably for some participants there will be sharing of data that would not arise in a one-to-one interview. In contrast, some participants will limit their sharing in a group situation. To account for such nuances it is worth considering using both methods, although do be aware that this would complicate the design, generate more data and thus lead to more work.

We have touched upon questionnaire construction in the previous chapter. In doing so we have highlighted how easy it is to construct a bad quantitative questionnaire, and qualitative questionnaires are much the same. When putting together the questions to be answered, individuals should carefully consider their wording. In qualitative research the aim will be to generate detailed answers, and a questionnaire may follow a similar pattern to a structured interview schedule. Respondents therefore need to be able to understand the questions and have enough space to complete their answers. It is also worth inviting people to offer metaphors, images or pictures as part of their qualitative questionnaires. As with any method of gathering data it can't hurt to try out (pilot) the tool prior to giving it out to your participants – if your trial group can't answer the questions, it's likely that your research group won't be able to either.

It is often surprising for counsellors to hear that there are bodies of literature around interviewing techniques and questionnaire development. However, these are huge topics in themselves and there is a wealth of information to sift through regarding each research method. A few of the excellent texts that we have found particularly useful are noted at the end of the chapter. Additionally, in pre-empting some of the questions that you may have, below we answer two of the most common questions that come up in the classes that we teach.

'How many participants is enough?'

The inevitable question that we are asked in class regarding qualitative research is 'How many participants is enough?' This may sound simple, and we truly wish we had a definitive answer, but it is wrapped up in a whole bundle of other factors. For example, if an individual is hoping to conduct a focus group looking at counsellor trainees' experiences of undertaking a course with an integrative focus (as is mentioned above), it would be expected that the student will find quite a few interested parties relatively easily (let's say between ten and twenty anyhow). This is because they are conducting the work at an academic institution that offers integrative counselling training. In contrast, an individual may hope to examine the helpful aspects of counselling reported by male survivors of sexual abuse. In this instance, it would be anticipated that this participant group would be much less common, and that some of the individuals who researchers have the potential to work with may be ruled out due to ethical considerations. Thus, in this instance, individuals may only be expected to gather the views of a small number of participants (possibly two or three, or even a single in-depth case study). What we hope to convey here is that it is by no means a simple decision, and the context of the subject matter plays a very important part in the final decision. Furthermore, the methods adopted will have an impact. For example, where, as a standard, we may suggest six to eight substantial (one hour) interviews as a norm, we would also look to a minimum of two focus groups that last approximately an hour and a half and consist of six to eight participants each. The chosen methodology may also have suggestions for the number of participants. For example grounded theory suggests eight to twenty people (McLeod, 2011), even though many studies use fewer, and interpretative phenomenological analysis (IPA), which is potentially more labour intensive than grounded theory, recommends approximately four for those newer to the approach (Smith, Flowers and Larkin, 2009).

'What is the best way to capture the data?'

Individuals conducting interviews or focus groups often ask, 'What is the best way to capture the data?' Some people opt for video recordings, some audio recordings and others rely upon field notes. Each of these techniques can be successful; however, we would encourage individuals to consider the rationale for their decision. For example, what would video recording the interview add to the data that would not be in an audio recording? Likewise, what may be missing from field notes taken both during the interview and at the end of it? Thus, audio recordings are recommended in most cases so as to provide a relatively complete account of the meeting. There may however be good reason for participants to opt out of being recorded due to the unease of having a hard copy of their words collected. Such issues, which have become more complex owing to technological advances, need researchers to be mindful of relevant issues and clearly outline what happens to any recordings/notes following the meeting.

Making sense of talk: data analysis

Probably the area of work that counselling trainees struggle with most is data analysis – what do you do with the data (interview transcripts, observation notes, etc.) when you have collected it? The numerous complex terms associated with this type of research often feel unwieldy or overly complex and lead to increasing anxiety levels. Thus, at a time when the novice researcher wants a step-by-step guide, they are often confronted with philosophical/epistemological musings of eminent researchers. Now, as advocated by others, we do not dismiss the importance of these debates:

> Paradigm issues are crucial; no inquirer, we maintain, ought to go about the business of inquiry without being clear about just what paradigm informs and guides his or her approach. (Guba and Lincoln, 1994: 116)

However, there is a time and place for them and we acknowledge that getting to grips with these issues can be a little like being thrown into the deep end of a turbulent pool. This seems particularly relevant to highlight given that many approaches of qualitative analysis follow very similar procedures – notably breaking apart the data into small components (often called codes, themes or meaning units) and then putting it back together. The final product comprises a coherent story of the data that should have some tangible use to the reader. It will usually revolve around a major topic and have a number of sub-themes that help to explain the phenomenon being examined.

So, you might ask, 'Why is the philosophical element necessary?' Answers can include: 1) academics like that sort of thing; 2) qualitative research often plays second fiddle to its quantitative cousin and therefore needs to prove itself to have a sound rigorous basis; and 3) there are important assumptions about the way that the world can be understood, enmeshed within the full theories. Realistically there is a truth in each of these and we would encourage individuals using a specific method of data analysis to explore this further. However, for practitioners who aim to inform their practice by reading research articles, it is unlikely that they will have a thorough understanding of all approaches. Likewise, students completing a small-scale piece of research are not likely instantly to decipher the philosophical nuances of qualitative approaches. Thus, a focus for those in training may be to gain a simple understanding of the different approaches to research that counsellors utilise (see Box 4 for a brief overview of a number of qualitative approaches to data analysis).

BOX 4

Brief descriptions of qualitative approaches of research (each with its own tradition of data analysis)

Thematic analysis 'is a method for identifying, analysing and reporting patterns (themes) within data' (Braun and Clarke, 2006: 79). This involves phases of: familiarity with the data, generating initial codes, searching for themes, reviewing themes, defining and naming themes and producing the report.

Grounded theory was a term coined by Glaser and Strauss (1967) to describe a form of data analysis and theory development. The theory is inductively developed from a systematic analysis of the data, rather than by formulating a hypothesis in advance, which would be tested against data which is collected. In grounded theory research, the

---

unfolding theory is constantly referred back to the data to ensure that it remains grounded in the experiences and accounts of the research participants.

Interpretative phenomenological analysis (IPA) aims to offer insights into how a given person, in a given context, makes sense of a given phenomenon. Usually these phenomena relate to experiences of some personal significance – such as a major life event, or the development of an important relationship. It has its origins in phenomenology and hermeneutics.

Heuristic research was developed by Clark Moustakas (1990). He describes the approach as 'a search for the discovery of meaning and essence in significant human experience ... It requires a subjective process of reflecting, exploring, sifting, and elucidating the nature of the phenomenon under investigation' (Douglas and Moustakas, 1985: 40).

Autoethnography is a form of autobiographical personal narrative that explores the writer's experience of life. It differs fundamentally from ethnography – a qualitative research method in which a researcher uses participant observation and interviews in order to gain a deeper understanding of a group's culture – in that authoethnography focuses on the writer's subjective experience rather than the beliefs and practices of others.

An important question to be considered when anticipating the method of data analysis to be used in a qualitative study is 'What method best suits the phenomena under investigation?' This point has been made earlier in this chapter when reflecting upon the broader choice of research design and, in much a similar way, it is important to remember that the method chosen to analyse the data should be congruent with the topic being researched. Of course, such matching of methods of data collection and analysis is potentially dependent on training in a wide variety of techniques, so that the student has a rich repertoire to choose from. However, all too often, research methods training is minimal, with perhaps only one or two sessions devoted to contrasting methods. Additionally, counselling trainers may only feel equipped to train students in those approaches with which they are familiar, so research topics may often be squeezed into the approach taught.

Counsellors should take some comfort that data analysis is not a mystery pursuit but rather something that they do as part of their everyday practice. Additionally, the philosophy of taking a bottom-up versus top-down approach to making sense of what their participants are saying is an equally familiar pursuit to the counsellor. If I adhere to a particular therapeutic paradigm I use this template to try to make sense of what my client is saying on a day-to-day basis (a top-down approach of organising the data into predefined categories). If I take a more pluralistic approach I might be more likely to work with the data and let the words of the client drive the various therapeutic procedures that I employ (a bottom-up approach). Certainly data analysis is a complex activity, and researchers often feel a duty of care to do justice to their participant's words in the work, but it is congruent with the everyday activities of a counsellor.

Moving on from the techniques adopted to make sense of the data, it is pertinent to consider what good-quality qualitative research is. Elliott, Fischer and Rennie (1999) offer the factors in Table 4 as being especially relevant for the publication of qualitative research studies. Not surprisingly many of these factors are also applicable to evaluating the quality of a quantitative research study.

Table 4   Evolving guidelines for publication of qualitative research studies in psychology and related fields

A	Publishability guidelines shared by both qualitative and quantitative approaches
1	Explicit scientific methods
2	Appropriate methods
3	Respect for participants
4	Specification of methods
5	Appropriate discussion
6	Clarity of presentation
7	Contribution to knowledge
B	**Publishability guidelines especially pertinent to qualitative research**
1	Owning one's perspective
2	Situating the sample
3	Grounding in examples
4	Providing credibility checks
5	Coherence
6	Accomplishing general vs. specific research tasks
7	Resonating with readers

Source: Table taken from Elliott, Fischer and Rennie, 1999: 220.

Although such quality-control guidelines need unpacking further, once again we would reiterate that many of the checks are common sense. For example, being transparent about the choice and implementation of methods feels somewhat intuitive for any research publication. Furthermore, in relation to qualitative research, reminding authors of the need specifically to situate themselves in relation to the data, provide examples from transcripts and be explicit about credibility checks do not seem to be concepts that come out of the blue in any way. The message to take from this is that qualitative research comes in all shapes and sizes. Those conducting and reading research therefore need to be aware of the pitfalls and be appropriately informed of the types of issues to consider when evaluating the quality of work.

The student voice: Matt Shorrock

As a mature student – who first studied research methodologies over fifteen years ago whilst undertaking my undergraduate psychology degree – a quivering part of me was quite daunted at the prospect of returning to academia and empirical research. The reasons were many and varied, but quite understandable and common for a mature student, and raised hot questions such as 'Can I really balance an established psychotherapy practice, a growing family, and an academic career?' and 'Has "psychology" advanced so far that I will never catch up?' However, to my surprise, one of my biggest fears was grounded more in a philosophical tension than anything else.

Thankfully, I was sufficiently excited and driven by another part of me that was thirsty for 'knowledge', and hungry for professional growth, and it was this positive energy that enabled me to confront my fears. It was only whilst designing and writing up an in-depth client case study as part of a Master's degree that I was able to understand and articulate my growing philosophical conflict. Modernism had taught me to quantify the experience of my clients, but this blindly disregarded a rich mine of 'data diamonds' that had emerged over the recent decade, within my clinical practice. After four years of mandatory personal therapy as part of my training as a transactional analyst psychotherapist, one simple truth had manifested, that we are all unique, unique without exception, and that a whole heap of 'data diamonds' are simply not generalisable across populations. Returning to university, and being greeted at the doors of post-modernism, I was relieved to discover vast halls where I could play with my 'data diamonds', show them off and validate their 'truth'.

I would also like to pick up on another point raised by the authors, one that particularly resonated within me: the temptation to choose qualitative research due to a fear of 'doing' quantitative research. Whilst I stand by my previous point, that quantitative research cannot and does not fully provide us with full 'knowledge' or 'truth' (as if we could ever achieve that!), it certainly has its place. I remember being struck by my own fear of quantitative research methodology at the beginning of my latest training on a Doctorate in counselling psychology. The 'fear' seemed to permeate most of my cohort, as we carefully processed our concerns openly. Our fears were not only about epistemological incongruence with our work, practice and being. At a much more pragmatic level, we were concerned that our quantitative skills had rusted over, beyond becoming workable ever again. It may provide some relief to some readers, that after a brief refresher we were back up and running again, and our fear of the statistic-wielding, number-crunching monster was allayed. As researchers, as *good* researchers, I concur that it is indeed 'not good enough' to avoid using one methodology over another, due to fear, incompetence or lack of confidence. Allow yourself to be impassioned by your research question, do what you need to do to 'skill-up', and your method of arriving at the 'answer' will instead be an exciting, fearless adventure.

Perhaps one of the most important points to bear in mind, raised by the authors, deserves reiteration – especially to those of you with full and active lives outside of your academic research careers. Even if you with never harboured any scare towards quantitative research, and have developed strong, proud and shiny skill-muscles in this area, don't choose qualitative methodologies believing it to be an easier option. I would go so far as to say, in my experience, the opposite is mostly true. Qualitative research commands a heavy investment of time as well as energy. If you choose qualitative methods, you most definitely need to be passionate about your chosen area of research as you will need to live and breathe the 'data' throughout the whole study. I can't say this will be true of all researchers, although I'm yet to come across one who at Master's or Doctoral level has engaged meaningfully with the qualitative process, and has *not* experienced moments (or periods) of overwhelm or exhaustion. Having said that, experience also tells me that the reward is commensurate with the investment, and is always worth it!

You may be aware, as you read (or hear?) my 'student voice', that I am modelling what it is to be a qualitative researcher. This parallel process wasn't entirely deliberate, as I wasn't sure what I wanted to write at the onset, except that I wanted to allow you to share the impact that reading this chapter (an intervention) has had on me. After reading the authors' input, I have consciously mined my own experience, and contacted memories, tacit knowledge, fantasies, feelings, urges, behaviour ... the list goes on. It has become a mini-heurist study (Moustakas, 1990) in its own right. I may not have given you any numbers but I have given you *my* 'truth', and that is worth something beyond what numbers could possibly represent.

And so, in concluding my thoughts, feelings and reflections, it is my humble view that post-modernism properly accounts and enables us to flex our qualitative, as well as quantitative muscles, as we mine for diamonds of 'truth' and 'knowledge'. The exponential growth, appreciation and validity of quantitative research methodologies have cleared the path to collect and make sense of 'talk, thoughts and feelings in research' in ways that are both meaningful and congruent with practising as scientist-practitioner miners.

Summary points

- Qualitative research proves a popular choice for many counselling trainees undertaking a piece of research. It consists of making sense of complex, naturally occurring information such as people's words, thoughts and feelings.
- Common qualitative research methods include one-to-one interviews, focus groups and qualitative questionnaires. Other approaches include observations and reflexive journaling.
- There are numerous practical, personal and ethical challenges to qualitative research – it is definitely not an easy option!
- Making sense of qualitative data often raises numerous anxieties for students. These can be (partly) dispelled by reiterating the common sense that lies behind the complicated words that authors often use.
- The data that is generated using qualitative approaches reflects local knowledge and cannot be readily generalised to larger groupings.
- Quality checks should be in place to ensure rigorous engagement with the data that has been generated. Those who conduct research and consume research (as interested readers or policy-makers) should be able to assess research quality.

FURTHER READING

Below we identify some of the texts about qualitative research that have proven useful within our own work and that of students. Specifically we outline one general text that we would recommend as a great overview of qualitative research and is directed specifically at counsellors and psychotherapists, before focusing upon specific research methods (with a view to generating data) and research methodologies (with a view to outlining how to analyse different types of data).

General

A fantastic introduction to the world of qualitative research in counselling and psychotherapy is John McLeod's text:

McLeod, J. (2011) *Qualitative Research in Counselling and Psychotherapy*, Second Edition. London: Sage.

Qualitative research methods

There are numerous methods for collecting qualitative data. Below we make reference to useful texts for some of the most common.

Interviews

Kvale, S. and Brinkmann, S. (2008) *InterViews: Learning the Craft of Qualitative Research Interviewing*, Second Edition. London: Sage.

Focus groups

Bloor, M., Frankland, J., Thomas, M. and Robson, K. (2001) *Focus Groups in Social Research*. London: Sage.

Qualitative research methodologies/data analysis

Here we stick to providing core texts related to those mentioned within this chapter.

Thematic analysis

Braun, V. and Clarke, V. (2006) 'Using thematic analysis in psychology', *Qualitative Research in Psychology*, 20 (3): 77–101.

Grounded theory

Corbin, J. and Strauss, A. (2008) *Basics of Qualitative Research: Techniques and Procedures for Developing Grounded Theory*, Third Edition. London: Sage.

Interpretative phenomenological analysis

Smith, J., Flowers, P. and Larkin, M. (2009) *Interpretative Phenomenological Analysis: Theory, Method and Research*. London: Sage.

Heuristic research

Moustakas, C. (1990) *Heuristic Research: Design, Methodology and Applications*. London: Sage.

Creative approaches to research (e.g. Autoethnography)

Etherington, K. (2004) *Becoming a Reflexive Researcher: Using Our Selves in Research*. London: Jessica Kingsley Publishers.

Speedy, J. (2008) *Narrative Inquiry and Psychotherapy*. London: Palgrave.

8

Ethical Issues in Therapy Research

Abstract

Hopefully by this point we have nearly convinced you (if not bored you with the mantra!) that therapists are well placed to enter the world of research, in terms of their methods of both collecting and also analysing data. A particular strength of the counsellor is their attention to ethical practice and their adherence to an ethical framework in the everyday practice that they undertake. This is the emphasis of this chapter. We first look to uncover the ethical considerations that inform your work with clients, and explore how these might apply to research settings. We then move on to consider the contextual requirements of undertaking a piece of research and the ethical clearance procedures that you are likely to be exposed to, either as part of an educational qualification or in terms of collecting data within your organisation. Duncan Craig, one of our past counselling trainees and now the service director of a counselling service, then provides a more personal reflection about engaging with ethical considerations whilst studying for a qualification. Furthermore, some key documents and texts are outlined at the end of the chapter for those wishing to follow up our discussions.

THOUGHT BOX 8

What does the word 'ethics' mean to you? And where do you encounter it in your therapeutic practice?

Consider:

- Do you adhere to an ethical framework?
- How might this translate to research issues?
- How might these ethical frameworks differ for therapy and research?

Ethical counselling practice and research

Counselling by its very nature needs to be ethical and fixed to an appropriate framework (such as BACP, BPS or HCPC – see the end of the chapter for references to these) in order for it to hold safely the work of both client and counsellor. The ways in which these will be played out however will be dependent on the context of your counselling practice. The overlap between therapeutic practice and research is considerable, and ethics is another area where the counsellor researcher will be in a strong position to understand the requirements for a research project to be ethically sound. We now move on to consider the ethical issues that are inherent to your practice and the ways in which these principles might or might not be transferred to research into therapy.

ACTIVITY 15: What does it mean to be an ethical professional?

When discussing ethical behaviour in everyday life there are fundamental rights and freedoms that we would hope for, for example that we respect others in a way that we would hope to be respected. Psychologists, counsellors and indeed researchers are in a position of authority and this needs to be attended to and addressed in the various professional relationships that we encounter in our work. Let's just stand back for a moment and reflect on the ethical principles that we bring to our practice. Often these can be so inherent in what we do that we can skim over their importance.

This activity attempts to:

1   remind you of the ethical underpinnings of your practice
2   encourage you to reflect upon why these considerations are important to your therapeutic work

and

3   help you to consider the extent to which these practices might transfer to the research arena.

The activity

In this activity we ask you to reflect on your therapeutic practice and to consider what the ethical principles are that guide your work. In a similar way we then ask you to consider the usefulness of these principles when undertaking research.

In the first task we ask you to reflect upon what ethical principles you work to as a counsellor or psychotherapist. In doing so, try not to get too hung up on ethical frameworks. Think about the nuts and bolts of your minute-by-minute practice in keeping you and your client safe in the work that you undertake together. Once you have done this then think how these actions fit into an ethical framework.

When this list is complete and you have noted down a thorough set of therapeutic principles, consider the ease with which these actions and principles might transfer to the world of counselling and psychotherapy research (Task 2). You might find it helpful to do this using a traffic light system where those practices that could be transferred with ease are marked up as green, those needing further consideration amber and those that would not transfer (as the activities of therapy and research are too different) are marked as red. Thinking in this way allows you to reflect critically on the use of ethics in your practice and research, so developing the critical voice that is so important in your final write-up.

ACTIVITY BOX 15

What does it mean to be an ethical professional?

Task 1: Being an ethical professional

Reflect upon what ethical principles you work to as a counsellor or psychotherapist. How do you take care of the client in your therapeutic work?

Task 2: Being an ethical counsellor researcher

How might these skills transfer to the world of research? Are there any areas that do not fit comfortably?

Your findings

We bet the first points that came to mind were general issues to do with consent, contracting and levels of confidentiality, all of which are important aspects of your work in fostering safety in the therapeutic setting. You might even have mentioned some ethical frameworks. But what do these mean in reality in terms of what you do with your client? Some of these skills might come so naturally to you now in terms of the care that you offer to your clients that you might barely notice them; it is worth taking a step back to really notice what you are doing in fostering this care and the trust that is referred to later in this section (Bond, 2000).

Read through the 'Our findings' section, which contains a summary of a desk-based piece of research reflecting upon several ethical frameworks, and consider how the concepts marry with what you do with your clients in creating a safe and ethical space for your practice.

Our findings

This section introduces you to the two most common frameworks that you will come across in research in this arena. These come from the British Psychological Society (BPS) and the British Association for Counselling and Psychotherapy (BACP).

Adhering to frameworks

As therapists, we are used to using models and theories to help to inform our work, although it is unlikely that we will force these upon a client's story in making sense of the material they bring to us in therapy. In a similar way, whilst our professional bodies have developed ethical frameworks to help support our thinking about client work, they are not intended to be read as a 'how to' guide. We must think about our actions in terms of ethical dilemmas, just as we think about client material and the use that we make, or do not make, of theoretical paradigms.

The two main ethical frameworks that you are likely to be familiar with in this area come from the BPS (2009) and the BACP (2010). It is not the intention of this text to describe each of the frameworks in turn; as noted above, these can be accessed via the resources listed at the end of this chapter. Both documents however cover similar territory, and the main points of consideration are listed below around the core issues of respect, competence, responsibility and integrity.

Respect

As in any therapeutic work, difference should be respected in a research encounter. Any information gleaned from a research interview should be dealt with respectfully in terms of its storage and maintenance of confidentiality. Informed consent should be sought, although special procedures apply with regard to children, detained people and those with significant impairments. Where real consent from the participants is not possible it should be accessed from those who are in the best position to understand the perspective of the potential participant. Additionally, associated power dynamics should be taken into account in these situations. The BACP speak of these issues in terms of trustworthiness, ensuring informed consent, honouring of the relationship and awareness of prejudice and risk.

In seeking informed consent in therapy, practitioners are likely to agree arrangements for payment and non-attendance, length of session, number of contracted sessions and agreed aims for the work. In so doing they are agreeing to work together, and in effect the client is giving their informed consent to take part in the work. 'Informed consent' in the world of therapy is a complex issue that deserves further discussion; suffice to say here that in any meaningful, therapeutic encounter it is often an uncertain enigma as to where the talk will go in deepening understanding. The extent to which informed consent is achievable in therapy is therefore debateable and it could be argued that surprises, uncertainties and unravelling are often part and parcel of good therapy (West, 2002). This has major implications for the counsellor as researcher. We invite counsellors to partake in research due to their skills of facilitation and, in so doing, we warn them too to be mindful of the boundaries between a research interview and therapeutic encounter. In boundarying this work, the research debrief becomes central.

Whilst always best to avoid deception, there are occasions where it is necessary to keep information from participants in research studies, and a debrief regarding any information that has been withheld should be offered at the earliest opportunity. Where deception is used, the researcher should have exhausted all other alternative designs and be clear about the impact that deception might have on the participant, and these should be considered in the context of the social and cultural background of potential participants. Even where no deception has been used, we should ensure that the participant is cared for and offered a debrief or referred on for further support if necessary. Related to this, when we ask for our trainees to list what they might want to look at for their theses and dissertations the list often makes for sad reading. Counselling is often a sad business, with people commonly seeking support when they are troubled, and therefore it makes sense that we will research into these topics. It is therefore necessary that when people partake in a research interview about these sensitive issues we prepare for follow-up support to be available, whilst also managing the research interview to be held within appropriate parameters.

As in therapy, all participants in a research study should be informed that they have the right to withdraw at any time, along with their data, irrespective of any incentive that has been offered. There are always power dynamics at play between researcher and participants and these should be attended to openly.

Competence

As in standard therapeutic practice, the BPS comments on levels of competence as an ethical standard. As we monitor our own fitness to practise as therapists in terms of personal and professional development, so we should monitor our fitness to practise in research endeavours. We should ensure that we are familiar with standards of good practice and appropriate ethical frameworks and ensure that we utilise appropriate supervision in our research work. Further, we should be sure that we are clear about the levels of confidentiality that we are able to offer both our clients in therapy and our participants in research. This information is subject to all data protection requirements, and the information shared by participants should remain confidential where possible. Where there are likely to be breaches of this, these should be clearly explained at the outset. This might cause particular issues for certain client groups and settings (e.g. work in a forensic setting). Any likely publication of the research should be explained and the participant assured that their data will be non-identifiable.

The BPS reminds researchers to be mindful of their role of researcher, and if anything causes concern regarding the emotional or behavioural wellbeing of the participant, they have a duty to feed this back to the participant. They need to be wary of offering any further advice unless qualified to do so or it forms part of the procedures agreed to earlier. Researchers also have an ethical duty to remind their colleagues of ethical practices in research.

Responsibility

We have a responsibility to our clients, the general public, to the profession and, in terms of research, to the world of science. Avoidance of harm must therefore be central to our work. In relation to research, there should be no greater risk to the participant from taking part in it than that which they may expect from their everyday life. An assessment of such issues should be independently considered (we discuss independent monitoring of research projects below). Furthermore, participants should be informed that they have the right to withdraw from the research at any point in time.

Integrity

We should be honest and accurate in our work as psychologists and counsellors and, in terms of research, we should be clear about the knowledge and skills that we bring to the work and the counter-arguments that could be made of our research findings. We should be aware too of the roles that we take in engaging in research work with participants and the limits that exist in terms of this role; the research interview should not be confused with a therapeutic encounter. As outlined above, whilst we bring our skills of therapist to the interview, we need to be clear where the research interview stops and where therapy might begin.

Discussion

Therapy is a messy business and hopefully your thoughts will have reflected this. Researching topics around therapeutic work it is likely to be messy too and probably should be if it is doing the job properly. Just as where good therapy 'holds' the messiness in terms of the ethical procedures that you put in place to keep it safe, a good piece of research should hold the messiness too in terms of its design, analysis, write-up, conduct and care of the participants. In terms of data collection (or you might have referred to it as what you do in your therapeutic hour) you know how to set a respectful environment in a designated space that is undisturbed. You know how to set up the working therapeutic environment for therapy or a research interview, the layout of chairs, and the clock or watch in your line of sight to ensure that you can keep your eye on it without it impacting on the work you undertake with your client. You know about non-verbals, prompts and respectful listening and the boundaries that you need to set in terms of levels of confidentiality in relation to risk for self or others. These are made clear at the start of the session so that the client can make an informed decision about their levels of sharing. These considerations serve to hold the client safely and in an ethical manner, and do the same in a research interview.

A research interview is a human encounter and when considering ethics our thoughts often turn to issues of dignity, justice and equality. The moment-to-moment things we do in our practice give evidence of our viewing the encounter as such. Often ethical frameworks can be seen as somewhat abstract so it is useful to consider what they mean to our everyday practice and how they are demonstrated to the client and evidenced – hence our invitation to you to think about what you actually do in therapy. Often, when asked to get into the frame of research, counsellors freeze, getting blocked by the jargon and complex language of the pursuit. By listing the skills that you use in therapy and then denoting them red, amber and green in terms of their transferability to research we can free ourselves up to see the counsellor as a well-skilled researcher. The everyday skills that you use in your therapeutic work therefore give an underpinning of respect and care to your research endeavours.

In summary, ethical principles are deeply engrained within an individual's therapeutic practice, indeed often they may be so deeply entrenched that we forget what we are doing because they come so naturally to us. We are in a good position to undertake research activities because of this, but we should be cautious. Research is not therapy, the tasks are different and people have engaged in conversation with us for different reasons; the parameters of the conversations should be set accordingly.

Researching therapy in an ethical manner

The section above has considered our practice as counsellors and psychotherapists and invited you to look at it as an ethical endeavour that can be transferred to the research arena. This is helpful to us in demystifying the often abstract meaning of 'ethics'. A landmark report by the National Commission for the Protection of Biomedical and Behavioural Research (1978) outlined the seven main principles of ethical research as:

Beneficence: Research is done to gain knowledge and illuminate the human condition. It is not done to cause harm to an individual or group. It ultimately aims at increasing understanding to promote opportunity, quality and enhancement.

Honesty: This is essential to the process of research. Integrity should be present within all stages of research projects (e.g. design, data collection, data analysis, dissemination).

Accurate disclosure and informed consent: Participants should be informed of the topic and procedures involved in the research. Where possible they must give their informed consent (there are special considerations with under-16s and certain clinical populations).

Confidentiality: It is expected that participants' data will remain anonymous and that special permission should be granted for this to be contravened.

Protection: Research participants should not be placed in danger and where personal or sensitive issues are to be discussed these should be considered carefully and participants should give their full consent.

Respect: Participants should be treated in a courteous way, including those who might not be autonomous, for example children.

Justice: Those who bear the risks in research are the ones who benefit from it; procedures should be reasonable, non-exploitative and fairly administered.

So, if these are pinnacles of what it means to undertake ethical research, what do they mean to us as we plan a piece of research?

ACTIVITY 16: How to research therapy in an ethical manner

As noted above, we now want to get you into more of a research mindset. In the first activity you considered what it is that you already do as therapists that might be useful in research activities. In this activity we explicitly ask you to consider how to research in an ethical manner. This might seem straightforward but do be mindful that we are all guided by numerous biases and self-preserving behaviours that might get in the way.

The following activity attempts to:

1   encourage the reader to plan a piece of research
2   help the reader to consider who to ask to participate and how to make sense of what they say

and

3   help the reader to consider how to undertake research in an ethical way.

The activity

Imagine you have to demonstrate your effectiveness as a practitioner, a common scenario in today's economic climate. How might you do it? In Activity Box 16 we provide a short scenario and ask you to respond to this by developing a brief strategic plan for the service in question. As you do this activity, be mindful of what motivates your decisions.

ACTIVITY BOX 16

How to research therapy in an ethical manner

You are a manager of a counselling service and your funders want you to produce a research report into the effectiveness of your service. How you do it is up to you. Your first job is to consider what the problems are in agreeing to this and how you might overcome them in an ethical manner – a tricky one as you are all therapists, with no experience of Research (with a big R)!

Consider the following:

- Who might you ask to participate?
- What information might you collect?
- Who might collect the information?
- How will you make sense of the information collected?

Your findings

What were the feelings generated in you by this proposed research project? Panic due to your lack of competence in undertaking research? Stress because of the fear that the conclusion of such a project might not reflect well on you in terms of your work? Were you worried about what the implications of such a piece of research might be? Will the audience (i.e. your funders) understand the complexities of how counselling operates and that, for example, scores demonstrating that people are getting worse might actually be a marker of later improvement? Did you panic about how you would fit such an evaluation into your already jam-packed work schedule? If so, then your thoughts reflect something of the stressed practitioners that we encounter in our classes, which reflect too the ethical considerations outlined above from the BPS and BACP.

Our findings

Below we introduce some of the common issues that arise in our class-based discussions around such a case scenario.

Who is going to be involved in the research?

We will just ask them – the clients, it's obvious!

If we want to know about therapy, who better to ask than the client? They might even be interested in the research because it connects with their particular concern; therefore we would get real data of meaning from the horse's mouth!

We need of course to remember that your client's main aim in therapy is to get better and any involvement in a research project is likely to contaminate the natural processes of therapy (possibly in a good way). Indeed, if you elected to look at how helpful therapy has been to them, you would need to be cautious about the answers given – they are likely to take a more (or less) favourable evaluation due to the power dynamics of your relationship, so compromising the validity of any conclusions reached.

We would also have to be confident enough of the client's psychological robustness to be in the study; even though they might have given their consent at the start of the work it might well unravel levels of data that are disturbing and unanticipated for the participant. The discussion is research and not therapy, so debriefing procedures and follow-on referral agencies would need to be outlined from the outset. Further, we have to be confident in the participant's ability to withdraw their participation from the study, again bearing in mind the power issues outlined above.

Some might argue that a more ethical position is to talk to clients after therapy has terminated, although a differing opinion could question the ethics of revisiting and scratching away at a scab that has healed, without the ongoing support of psychological therapy.

Agreement

They should agree to it; we mustn't force them to be involved.

Research participants should have given their agreement to involvement in the research and should have been briefed as fully as possible about the aims of the project, but how will we truly know what might ensue in the research interview and the paths that the conversation might take? (As Einstein was once noted as saying: 'If we knew what it was we were doing, it wouldn't be called research, would it?') It's just like therapy, and a form of process consent as well as an initial agreement would need to be used.

What about if it is so obvious what we are researching that making it clear to the participant might result in their saying exactly what they thought we were looking for? Might there be occasions when we don't want to tell the participant everything about the study to see what they would naturally do? How unethical is it to deceive them? Protocols should be developed that allow for appropriate debriefing at the end of the study.

Withdrawal

We should certainly allow the participant to withdraw should they want to. And they should be able to take their data along with them.

But what about if you elect to conduct a group interview – how easily could they withdraw because of group pressures and would they really be able to take their data with them? For example, if X says something followed by Y and then Z, and then Y decides to remove themself from the study, their contribution is struck out and yet their presence still remains as a link between the contributions of X and Z. This gap would need to be commented on and so really their data is still there in some way! This is a potential nightmare!

Non-maleficence

How competent are we to undertake this research in the first place? I don't know anything about research, let alone research with a big R!

The counselling researcher may only receive a term's input on research methods, whereas their counselling psychology colleague will have three years' training and that's just at undergraduate level. What does this mean for our research participants? One would hope that the counsellor researcher has a deeply informed set of skills and standards that have developed as part of their practice as counsellor; however, these need honing and reframing to some extent. This is the focus of this chapter – a delicate acknowledgement of your skill in research and recognition of its difference from practice.

What about the psychological impact on me as the researcher? If we look at something that matters then it is likely to have an impact upon me as the researcher, particularly as I talk to other people about all sorts of feelings, hunches and emotions. Can I write this into the report? It feels like important information to me, though I don't think that counts as big-R research – but how unethical is it to leave it out?

These considerations need to be harnessed in an appropriate research design and this is introduced elsewhere in this text, but the emotional impact of this passion and the self-care of the researcher within it needs to be catered for. Again counsellors are well used to this in terms of their use of their everyday professional practice (e.g. attending to processing material, supervision and time-out from client work). There are further issues in relation to training in the extent to which the counsellor trainer feels competent in research methods when their preferred allegiance lies with practice, thus the need for a book such as this to support them in this work!

Anonymity

We need to keep names out of the work – surely? It needs to be an anonymous report. But the client group that we work with is tiny.

This can be difficult as counselling is a small world and in some very specific or unusual studies the potential research population is small. Therefore, even though data contained within any report would be anonymous there might still be the potential for the participant or their peers to recognise the respondent. Indeed, often the most powerful, unique data that we want to contain within a report can be particularly identifiable!

How do I make sense of what people say to me with integrity?

Isn't research about finding answers to things? Conclusions? How can I decide what the conclusions are to anything we decide to look at? How do I decide what to take notice of and what to leave out in reaching my conclusions?

If people have given up their time, thoughts and feelings to take part in a research project there is a duty on the part of the researcher to handle the data with integrity and to do their best to represent the 'truth' of what the participant was sharing. This is often the point that the counsellor researcher particularly struggles with. These are issues of the validity/trustworthiness of our findings and there are a variety of methods that can be adopted to check the accuracy of our conclusions (as briefly introduced in Chapters 6 and 7). Often the counselling researcher feels a heavy duty of responsibility that can lead them to drown in interview data. The need to emerge with both ethical and accurate conclusions can prove disabling and the counsellor researcher should remember that they are not alone in their endeavours.

Often an inherent dislike is felt of 'doing something' to the voices of the participants. In particular, reducing the conversations to themes or even numbers can be uncomfortable and this can result in interesting decisions regarding methodological choices and methods of analysis. However, whatever the decisions, the counsellor has elected to take on the role of researcher and they need to do something with the information that has been shared. The counsellor researcher has an ethical responsibility to make a shift in what they do with the data, the way that it is presented in the final report and its final dissemination. All too often research projects result in graduation for the student and end up collecting dust in university libraries rather than developing knowledge and practice. Let's not forget that participants have come along to the meeting in the hope their data will be used, made sense of in an appropriate and respectful way, and added to the pot of previous research literature to ultimately move knowledge forward.

Discussion

As counsellors and psychotherapists we find ourselves working in a multitude of contexts. Whilst the BACP and BPS see research activities as central to our work and helpful in informing our practice, it can often be difficult getting the permissions necessary to undertake a small piece of research such as the one described above in this activity. It is interesting to consider that some of the classic research studies that tell us most about human behaviour are often those studies which are most troublesome in terms of ethics; think for example of the studies of obedience by Milgram and Asch's work on conformity (Twenge, 2009, and Rozin, 2001, respectively). This is work that is still on GCSE, A-level and undergraduate psychology syllabuses as the findings, though unnerving, remain observations that we can recognise in relation to our own behaviour. They have a resonance; they tell us something about the darker side of the human condition and, in so doing, we hopefully learn something to make society a better place. Yet, it is difficult to know whether these studies would have been given ethical clearance today.

In summary, the above sections outline the ethical dilemmas that counsellors often face when researching their work. These echo the concerns that the BPS and BACP outline in their ethical frameworks, which emphasise our need to 'think' and 'engage' with ethics, rather than looking towards the frameworks as providing 'shoulds' and 'musts'. Research is a complex business and therefore it is useful to have some sort of independent auditing procedure to ensure the ethical safety checks that we put into place in our work. Ethics committees are becoming more and more familiar within organisations undertaking research; it is to them that we finally turn.

The ethics committee

If you plan to undertake any piece of research, it is likely that you will encounter an ethics committee at some point in your journey. This might be at your academic institution or from the host institution where you intend to collect your data, for example the NHS or the prison service.

Broadly speaking there are three pathways into which your research project will fall: 1) secondary research; 2) practice review or service audit; 3) primary research (terms which might shift slightly in different settings). In secondary research, data is derived from published sources and therefore the potential for 'leakage' of personal data is negligible; consequently the procedures that you will need to follow for clearance for this type of research will be accordingly simple and minimal. The other two pathways get rather more troublesome and their distinction is somewhat blurred. Practice review or service audit requires a 'lighter touch' in terms of ethical clearance than primary research, because these types of studies are seen to be research activities which would form part of the practitioner's everyday work, but with the data being harnessed and reviewed in a formal way. Often reports generated from this sort of work will remain in-house, whereas primary research results in publications that have a much broader audience – potential for leakage is therefore greater and so consequently procedures for ethical clearance will be weightier.

Often the ethical clearance procedures that you encounter, for example at a university, will follow those of the NHS. This produces a problem for the social sciences as we will feel a pressure for our research questions and designs to follow the templates of the medical model. We said earlier that the world of therapy is messy, and working to this sort of template can sometimes feel as though we are pretending to fit a square peg into a round hole. There are further problems with ethics committees. On the surface it makes inherent sense that some initial quality check is made of a research plan, whilst others argue that the initial plans that are presented do not portray the complexities anyway of the actual research process (e.g. Hammersley, 2009). Clearance procedures allow for an explicit, organised consideration of the planned project although it is unlikely that they will iron out the complex tensions of researching some of the more complex phenomena of human nature (Cloke et al., 2000). It might well be because the business of counselling is messy that institutions struggle with rubber stamping rather more qualitative approaches, hence their preference might be towards a more medical model of research due to their increased perceived levels of accountability.

On a practical level ethics committees might result in some research not taking place. You will have a deadline for any research you undertake, and for the student who wants to collect data from within the NHS, they will have to complete their ethical protocols and this will impact on their university timescales; unfortunately, but understandably, if this is too lengthy, the result might often be that they choose to undertake another study. Universities equally have their own sets of procedures which again inevitably eat into writing-up time; all too often these procedures are themselves relatively new and students may opt for more mainstream topics and methodologies in order to get through panels more easily. Either way, there is a sense that although needed, one of the inevitabilities might be that clearance procedures may be censoring what is researched or that the researcher feels less inclined to research the more troublesome aspects of human behaviour, those aspects to which we should be attending to most.

The student voice: Duncan Craig

I can remember feeling completely overwhelmed when I first learned I would have to seriously consider the ethical issues attached to my research. I can recall how in a single moment this one word produced a tsunami of anxiety, in truth shared by the majority of students in that lecture room, and momentarily removed any scrap of confidence I had begun to build in my ability as a researcher.

'Ethics' is a word I'd often associated with medical research or psychiatry and believed to only be applied to those carrying out 'experiments' in a laboratory or hospital. I'd not thought 'ethics' applied to my work, nor did many of my fellow student researchers. But whilst discussing the 'questionable' interventions of a practitioner with my therapy supervisor, I recognised a word often used within our supervision sessions:

> 'you get annoyed when others are not practising in a way you believe is **ethical**, because that goes against everything you believe.'

I made a connection I hadn't before – as a therapist I am already dealing with ethics and have been since I began training! I am a member of the BACP, and have been since being a student, and like all members I agree to adhere to and work within the Ethical

Framework for Good Practice in Counselling and Psychotherapy. The third principle of the framework is 'Beneficence' – *'a commitment to promoting the client's well-being'* (BACP, 2010: 3) – and this can only be agreed to by practising ethically. We consistently use reflective thinking skills in everyday practice, as therapists, to ensure we are acting with beneficence. It's these very same skills that are used in research practice to ensure ethical issues are considered and appropriately addressed. **It's just a continuation of acting in the best interest of the client whilst causing no harm, within one's own competency, in order to promote understanding.** Once the connection was made the anxiety attached to dealing with 'ethics' in my research gradually dispersed and my confidence re-grew.

I meet all research ideas, plans or proposals with the same mindset now and the first question I always ask is *'How will the findings of this research help?'* If the justification for carrying out the research isn't ethically sound then I must question why one is doing it in the first place! I decided to ask a fellow student to actively criticise and make comment on the 'what', 'why' and 'how' of my research proposal in order for me to create rebuttals and justify my decisions. This task helped me reflect on my lines of thinking and the foundations to my logic; so much so that I changed two significant elements of the research design after selected elements were highlighted as being 'ethically questionable'. This is a practice I continue to do now and would absolutely recommend any reader do the same.

The process also highlighted what I now see as the second most important ethical consideration – 'safety of the researcher'. My own research focused on an issue extremely personal to me, one I had discussed within my own therapy, so I had to ask myself the question *'How will this enquiry affect me?'* and other such questions as *'What plans do I have to ensure I am fit to practise?'* If this exploration was believed to potentially have a negative impact on my wellbeing, regardless of how important to 'the greater good' I think the question is, then clearly it would be unethical for me to carry out this project – I am clearly not the right person to be conducting this research. **I do not think that it gets any more complicated than that**. As a therapist, I would not work in an area that would cause me harm, as this would cause me not to be fit to practise. Therefore the same principle has got to apply in the practice of research.

Going through my research proposal and work plan with a fine-tooth comb during this process, questioning every minute detail, also helped with ease of completing the University Research Ethics Committee (UREC) form. It enabled me to know my research 'inside out' and therefore congruently to answer all the questions on the form with as much detail as possible. However, whilst answering the questions on the form I did find that I needed to generate further documents and evidence to give the ethics committee more detail, such as the body copy for all letters and emails I would be sending to organisations to request their support in my appeal for participants. So in learning from this experience and observing the experiences of others, in future, I would build into my schedule an extra two days to complete all the necessary paperwork attached to carrying out research. Trust me on this: the process takes a lot longer than people hope or expect. But the more time taken at the front end of the research project means you will be better prepared for what I felt was the biggest hurdle to overcome – the 'ethics committee' interview.

As my research proved potentially contentious I had to attend an ethics committee meeting to answer any questions they had about my proposal. I don't think anyone can truly prepare you for the first time you walk into a room and sit in front of ten people who are potentially about to 'rip your proposal apart'. Sat in the corridor outside the committee room like the 'naughty schoolboy waiting to see the headmaster' filled me with so much nervous energy. Although this was the first time I sat waiting for the interview it was the third time that the ethics committee had taken up room in my consciousness, having twice previously been told to expect to be sent an interview date and time which never came to pass due to university systems. I sat there feeling that I was about to have my power drained from me, and questioning how ethical are ethics committees? But I kept thinking about the words of encouragement of my research supervisor and how I had pretty much gone through this process already with the fellow student mentioned earlier. I had also discussed the proposal in length in both therapy supervision and with my research supervisor, so there wasn't anything I didn't know about my proposal: I knew it inside out. So bring it on, committee, just try me! I say that partially with my tongue pressed firmly in my cheek but also with a useful bit of hindsight. If you have really done your preparation and you have genuinely been living and breathing ethics, then any 'amendments' or 'comments' the ethics committee make should only ever be minute or as part of a discussion for the purpose of clarification. The initial fear attached to the build-up to attending an ethics committee interview is much greater than the event itself. I actually found it quite an anti-climax to be honest and I know I won't feel anywhere near as nervous next time as I did then.

Finally, I want to make sure that the words in my 'student voice' do not lead you to believe you should only need be concerned with ethics at the beginning, during the planning or up to obtaining ethical approval, because that would be incorrect.

Acting in the best interests of your participants, project and data collected must be a continuous process – this is what it really means to consider the ethics of your research.

The primary author of this chapter (CL) references West's (2002: 263) words, *'The extent to which informed consent is achievable in therapy is debatable'*, and I would argue that the same applies in research. For the purposes of retaining anonymity and to create an environment conducive to collecting the fullest of answers, I chose not to collect any identifying information. But as I had no contact with my research participants, how could I be 100 per cent sure that informed consent was being applied in every case? The simple answer is that I couldn't. No one could. But then how is that ethical? Well I could reduce the risk as much as possible by creating a pathway that each potential participant had to go through, providing them with as much detail as I could before their agreeing to participate, and ensuring they had access to further sources of support. Additionally, I could make it easy to withdraw participation at any point in the data collection period. This latter point came alive when, for whatever reason, participant(s) chose to only answer initial sections of the questionnaire. Such an occurrence did however cause ethical considerations of its own – for example, what do I do with this incomplete data? For me, a decision to omit it from the main analysis was made. This was based on the idea that participants had chosen to disengage and therefore no longer wished to consent. Others may, however, come to a different conclusion.

I've realised that ethical considerations aren't something you 'do' at the beginning of a project, they are a process that continues throughout the lifespan of your work. They also do not just apply to a single project but throughout our work as therapeutic practitioners and researchers.

Summary points

- Counsellors are well versed in ethics and these skills are largely transferable to research.
- Counsellor researchers need to be clear of what hat they are wearing. A research interview about therapy is not therapy, however well skilled you are as a counsellor.
- Ethical frameworks are not 'shoulds' and 'musts' – they invite us to think about their application on a case-by-case basis.
- It is likely that any formal piece of research will be scrutinised by an ethics committee; there are pros and cons to the existence of these procedures.

FURTHER READING

The following are likely to be of use for a more general consideration of ethics in research:

Matthews, B. and Ross, L. (2010) *Research Methods: A Practical Guide for the Social Sciences*. Oxford: Pearson Education.
Somekh, B. and Lewin, C. (2005) *Research Methods in the Social Sciences*. London: Sage.

More specifically in relation to research and practice in counselling, do ensure that you are familiar with the codes of conduct from your professional body, which are often free to download. For example:

British Association of Counselling and Psychotherapy (2010) *Ethical Framework for Good Practice in Counselling and Psychotherapy*. Leicestershire: BACP.
British Psychological Society (2009) *Code of Ethics and Conduct*. Leicester: BPS.
Health and Care Professions Council (2008) *Standards of Conduct, Performance and Ethics*. London: HCPC.

Further reading around ethics in counselling research can be found in:

Bond, T. (2000) *Standards and Ethics for Counselling in Action*, Second Edition. London: Sage.
Bond, T. (2004) 'Ethical guidelines for researching counselling and psychotherapy', *Counselling and Psychotherapy Research*, 4 (2): 10–19.
British Psychological Society (2010) *Code of Human Research Ethics*. Leicester: BPS.
McLeod, J. (2009) *An Introduction to Counselling*, Fourth Edition. Maidenhead: Open University Press.

9

Talking about Research and Dissemination

Abstract

Now that we have considered the context and some of the methodological dilemmas associated with undertaking counselling research, we move on to consider issues to do with dissemination. Some would argue that if research is to be ethical then you as a researcher are duty bound to spread the word of your participants in order to develop practice and ultimately client outcome. This chapter therefore reflects upon the different avenues of dissemination and the processes involved in getting research into a more public domain. In turn we consider the following questions: 1) 'Where do we find out about new developments in counselling and psychotherapy?' 2) 'What do we need to consider when writing up our research?' 3) What makes a *good* therapy researcher?' and 4) 'Where might *your* research go?' These questions are interspersed with activities that purposefully encourage the reader to reflect upon key issues in this area and are developed by presenting reflections from the experiences of our student groups. Reflections about the chapter are then presented by Susan Dawson, an experienced counsellor and narrative researcher, before proactively encouraging you to consider how you will continue your discussions about research when you have finished reading this book.

THOUGHT BOX 9

How confident would you feel talking about research?

Consider:

- Is it something you could do with ease?
- What would stop you talking about it?
- Has this book helped?

Writing THIS book

If we reflect personally on the questions posed in Thought Box 9, we feel relatively confident in talking about research. First, we are all individuals who have conducted research and have relevant academic qualifications. Second, we have also agreed to write the text you are now reading! However, we are guessing that a majority of the readers of this text will not feel quite so confident or will, as indicated in other chapters, still be fearful of the world of counselling and psychotherapy research – although having said that, we do hope that by this stage of the book you do feel a little more positive. Before moving on we thought it would be useful to briefly share some of our experiences of pulling this text together. Imagine if you will the following conversation:

> Terry: Now, Chapter 9, that's a bit of a muddled mess. [Quickly backtracking] I mean … it's a good start, but I think it needs harnessing quite a bit.
>
> Clare: Yes I know it needs work, but this is where I'm up to and the deadline's tomorrow!
>
> William: Now I was writing my blog the other day …
>
> Clare and Terry: William!!!
>
> Clare: So what are we going to do with it?

Now this wouldn't be too far from the truth (we were actually well beyond the deadlines that had been set, but don't tell any of our students), but it also highlights an important point: it is one thing knowing and understanding something, but it is a whole different ball game communicating it to others. In pulling this book together, we found it incredibly challenging to create an appropriate format. That included deciding upon the content, the number of exercises, the writing style and so on – AND we hadn't even considered that we had to direct it at a particular audience. By now you'll have a sense of whether we have succeeded in our task or not. We're also guessing that some of you will like what we've created and some of you won't ('I found it a very informative and easy read' or 'I found it a bit too dumbed down and patronising'). In a similar way, if you look through the research into counselling and psychotherapy there will be bits that you warm to and bits that you detest with a passion. In the activities within this chapter we hope to get you thinking about how people write research and why they do it in the way that they do. However, before we do that, let's consider the different arenas in which we hear about new developments in counselling and psychotherapy.

ACTIVITY 17: How do you research *your* profession?

In this next activity we hope to outline some of the different ways that individuals keep themselves informed about developments within the world of counselling and psychotherapy. Often a major hurdle for some practitioners is that they do not know where to look in the first place, and we hope to convey the message that there are plenty of opportunities out there when you start looking.

This activity attempts to:

1 help you to think about where you find out about your profession
2 encourage you to reflect upon the different sources of information about developments within the therapeutic profession

and

3 help you to identify areas that you might be able to utilise to keep your practice up to date.

The activity

This is a simple reflective activity in which we ask you to write down a brief list of the places in which you might encounter counselling and psychotherapy research. This can be as broad and varied as you wish – in fact, do try to think about some of the less standard avenues you might go down, as these can often be the most fun.

ACTIVITY BOX 17

How do you research *your* profession?

Write down a brief list of places in which you might encounter information that helps you develop as a practitioner.
    Consider:

- Hopefully by this point you will feel rather more Research savvy (unless we haven't done our job!) but go back to thinking about research with a small r. Where do you find out about things to do with your professional practice? Where do you research what you are doing?

Your findings

You probably thought immediately about talking to colleagues about their practice and information that you glean from case conferences or case discussion. It is also likely if you are a student on placement that you made some considerable mention of what you learn on your training programmes in relation to personal development, skills work and theory. But which sources do you turn to in order to find out more in each of these areas?

What did you think about reading research, or those activities more commonly associated with big-R Research activities? If you are a member of the BACP the publications *Therapy Today* (the organisation's professional publication) and *Counselling Psychotherapy Research* (*CPR*: the organisation's research journal) will land on your doorstep. How convenient! But, do you read them? Counsellors are often quoted as saying that *CPR* remains in the plastic wrapping and that *Therapy Today* is opened because it more accurately reflects the work that practitioners are undertaking. Where do you stand on your reading material?

More proactively, have you attended a research conference? If so, which one and did you find it useful?

Finally, you might have considered how you research and understand your own therapeutic work. In this case what do you do to understand your practice better?

Our findings

The places that come to mind when discussing this with our students are pub discussions (feel free to replace with an alternative venue of choice), reading research and talking about research at conferences. Let's now consider these in more detail.

The pub

Counselling is by its very nature a private activity, but don't you sometimes wonder what other people are doing? What does your colleague, who you rate so highly, do to warrant your admiration? What is it in his or her practice that you rate? It is likely to be only in training that you are able to observe other people's work directly, so learning from their technical skills and critique of practice. But even then, what about other aspects of their training that are not talked about? Have you ever wondered what is happening in the personal development group in the training room next door to yours? How does their facilitator facilitate the group? You have always thought that you would much prefer to be in the group next door – you felt it worked 'better' than your group did. But what does 'work' mean – what are they getting up to in there and does your fantasy match what is actually happening? You might even have wondered about whether everything that happens in counselling is ethical – how do we know, as it is so hidden? For instance, to use the same example noted above, you are not supposed to talk about personal development groups outside of the group so how could you check out the ethical implications of some of what goes on? It is possible that you have brought this up with your tutors, but highly likely that you brought it up with your training colleagues over a coffee or a pint!

Reading research

A plethora of research journals related to counselling and psychotherapy exist (see the reference list at the end of this text for numerous examples) and the emphases of these vary, along with the extent to which you may or may not feel that they are relevant to practice. We outlined above how counselling can be a lonely activity and it is unfortunate that practitioners often feel research to be a totally different world for them, because research papers can offer information and support in developing therapeutic practice. As outlined in earlier chapters, the language that research is sometimes presented in can be off-putting, but this is not always the case and many journals are directed with the practitioner in mind.

Conferences

Where better to talk about what you do than at a conference? At the end of this chapter we consider how best to prepare your research for presentation at a conference, although we recognise that this might be a daunting endeavour. With this in mind, we have been instrumental in developing a student research conference at our university as a place for students to 'cut their teeth' in terms of conference presenting, and students often move on from this venue to a larger national or international conference. This is often accompanied by their writing of a journal article. As we outline below, it is often possible from a set of PowerPoint slides to prepare a paper for publication.

Discussion

Now let's begin with the sad reality. Believe it or not, although research is available in the places listed above, it is often not the most influential component to developing our practice. A survey of over 4,000 psychotherapists, who differed in terms of professional background, career level, theoretical orientation and nationality, found that contact with clients, practice supervision and personal therapy proved more influential on their development than the impact of research (see Orlinsky et al., 2001). Thus, with this in mind, we do not expect you to find research in the above places and change your practice overnight to being driven by this new fount of knowledge. In fact, although some individuals would support such a notion, we personally feel that research should only act as one part of the decision-making process in therapy – such a view can often be described as 'research-informed' rather than 'research-driven' (e.g. Bohart, 2005; Hanley et al., 2012). We do however hope that outing some of these resources might help individuals to become more informed consumers of research (e.g. Wheeler and Elliott, 2008).

In terms of everyday conversations about research, it seems a shame that at any one time in an academic institution there is likely to be a large body of counselling and psychotherapy trainees yet, due to the timings of the courses and the fact that they are often busy professionals, the opportunities for them to come together are limited. We try informally to link students up who are interested in the same research areas but this is not always logistically possible. Email and online resources therefore have become invaluable to foster this type of communication. In addition to this we formed a counselling research group that met on a quarterly basis to encourage dialogue between students (see Hanley and Lennie, 2008, for a brief discussion of this). Students made bids for a section of the evening, whether this was to present some findings or a chapter for feedback, pilot a questionnaire or to hear a keynote speaker. We tried also to make it a fun event with drinks and nibbles. Once we held the event on Valentine's Day, calling the meeting 'Falling in Love with Research', serving sparkling water (supposed to be champagne!), strawberries and chocolate lips! Obviously this is all very jokey but it did create energy around research and certainly fostered a community spirit in the counselling department.

These are conversations and thoughts that are probably familiar to you. Due to the hidden nature of the work, research is probably more important in counselling than in other disciplines. How else could we learn about what is actually happening in practice, training and supervision?

What do we need to consider when writing up our research?

So, now that we have considered where we might turn to find out about our profession, let's move on to think about you writing and disseminating your own research.

The writing-up process is part of what takes your musings in a coffee bar or pub to a different level. People have now elected to talk to you, knowing that their comments will be collated as part of a research project, whether it is a dissertation or research paper. You are ethically obliged now to add their views to the research literature that surrounds your area of investigation and thus enter into conversations around your topic. What is up to you is whether that discussion forms part of presenting your findings in relation to previous literature in a dissertation, writing a paper and publishing in a journal, or presenting at a conference and sharing a glass of wine and conversation with fellow colleagues before the inevitable post-conference festivities/embarrassment of disco jiving and karaoke begin!

So, let's now begin to consider that you have chosen to write up a research project on your topic of 'Taboo in Supervision'. But before we do this too heavily, let's consider karaoke for a little while …

MUSICAL INTERLUDE 1

Think back to when you last did karaoke (if you ever have done). Did your voice feel alone, weird, like it was standing out on its own and all out of tune? Strange when you had elected to sing a song you know so well, often imagining that you do actually sound like, well for me (CL), Marc Almond singing 'Tainted Love'. Why is this? Well clearly your voice is alone, and research is much the same. Say something on your own and you will feel timid, isolated and wonder 'Is it just me?'

For example, a lone counsellor's voice might say that they keep secrets from their supervisor – how unusual is this? Surely there are other voices that could sing the same song, so that the person doing the singing could gain in confidence to share some more and to understand the phenomenon further, resulting in an improvement of practice. This is about dissemination and locating your research in the research of others, i.e. developing voices and conversations. Perhaps you might go to a conference, hear something that strikes a chord, and this might facilitate your sharing in the bar later, indeed perhaps your research ideas for a paper or dissertation. The taboos of what is unsaid become said so that voices aren't so alone and we become more informed by hearing them.

When considering lone voices, some research methods attempt to facilitate individuals coming together. For instance, a well-functioning focus group can often be a really fruitful approach to disclosure in others because person A hears the responses of person B and that either stimulates further thought or develops their confidence to make 'riskier' disclosures, thus taking the discussion into unknown territory and providing rich data. However, such creative discussion and meanderings can lead to interesting questions about the storyline of the thesis or dissertation. Indeed, this chapter is an example of such a dilemma: there was an inherent drive to get key thoughts down on the paper, but arranging this into a coherent storyline was for some time lacking (and at this point I have to thank Terry for some excellent writing supervision in this regard!).

The importance of a clear research question to a successful and robust study, write-up and presentation cannot be over-emphasised. As mentioned in Chapter 7, your research question is like the lettering in a piece of Blackpool rock. It will drive what the literature is and how you locate your work alongside the writing of others. It will dictate what you say in the methods section about how you elected to collect information from which to answer your question. Finally, it will help you organise how you present your findings and discuss them in the light of the original literature, problems, implications and further research. We consider this more thoroughly when we turn to writing up the dissertation, but suffice to say Terry did exclaim at one point in this process of writing, 'We are still searching for the Blackpool in Clare's chapter!'

How do you write research up?

For reasons that have been considered throughout this text, undertaking a piece of research often triggers considerable anxiety in counselling and psychotherapy students. We hope you are now no longer feeling such angst! However, let's just take you back into your concerns once again. Consider for a moment what your worries would be regarding writing up a dissertation.

ACTIVITY 18: What makes a *good* counselling researcher?

Now, this is a loaded activity with a poor research question. Earlier on we invited you to consider what the 'best' approach to therapy is and the complexities around this question. Here the term 'good' is clearly equally at fault; however, hopefully this activity will give you some food for thought. Thus, we will ask you to identify someone you admire in the world of counselling and psychotherapy research, who you have read about or met, and reflect upon how they got to where they are today.

This activity attempts to:

1 encourage you to consider who the leaders are in counselling and psychotherapy research at the present time
2 support you in reflecting upon what your weaknesses might be when writing up research

and

3 help you to develop strategies for overcoming the challenges you might encounter whilst writing up research.

The activity

This is a three-part activity in which you will need something to capture your thoughts (e.g. pen and paper, laptop). To start we want to get you into the minds of people who are already producing high-quality research. In doing so, we ask you to identify someone from the world of therapy research with a view to outlining their motivations for undertaking research and the strengths that you perceive in them. We ask you to construct a brief vignette about this person to help you get into their way of creative thinking. We then ask you to consider the challenges that you imagine you will encounter whilst writing up your research, and finally to consider how your chosen researcher would address these challenges. Your thoughts around these issues become the second part to your story.

ACTIVITY BOX 18

What makes a *good* counselling researcher?

Task 1

Write a short vignette about someone you view as a successful researcher. Include in your story a reflection of why that person has undertaken the research they have and what strengths you see in them.

Task 2

Consider:

• What are *your* challenges when writing up a piece of counselling research?

Task 3

Return to the story you constructed in Task 1. The person you selected encounters the challenges you encountered in Task 2. What might this individual do to overcome these challenges? Add this component to your story.

Your findings

If we begin with the first of the tasks noted in Activity Box 18, did you come up with any names of counselling and psychotherapy researchers that you admire (or at least feel are skilled at what they do)? You may have considered the likes of professors Mick Cooper, Robert Elliott, Kim Etherington, Clara Hill, Michael Lambert, John McLeod, Bruce Wampold, Sue Wheeler and Carla Willig (selected with no criteria in mind and presented in alphabetical order). Each of these has been greatly influential in their particular areas and would easily have merited a mention in this context. You may have cited their achievements in books or papers written, the management of significant research projects, their humility and so on.

The second task that we asked you to complete moved to consider the challenges that *you* might encounter when writing up research. Were the issues personal, practical or even professional? So many things seem able to get in the way and people can easily be put off by such hurdles.

The final task asked you to reflect upon how you would imagine a good counselling and psychotherapy researcher would overcome your challenge – for instance, 'What would Mick Cooper do?' This is likely to be quite subjective and so we will leave you to consider this in your own time (possibly in personal therapy). We hope that it might help you to develop your own strategies to utilise when confronted by writer's block.

Our findings

Here we skip past our findings from the first task. Throughout this text we have referred to individuals that we have enormous amounts of respect for – they are all potential candidates here. As we reach Chapter 9 of this particular textbook, we will however highlight our admiration for their staying power with the task at hand!

In summarising the challenges that individuals face when writing up research, comments from our teaching groups are summarised below:

Struggling and juggling: Work, life, practice, relationships.

Encountering the research/practitioner divide: Making research relevant to practice.

Motivation: The ups and the downs of writing research.

Confusion: What am I doing? Or, why can't I understand what others have done?

Belief: Can I really do it?!

Feeling alone: The isolation of writing up research.

Changing tack: Disappointment on not finding what you want to.

Developing an academic voice: How do I write myself into the study? Am I allowed to?

Discussion

Let's begin by returning to the question 'What would Mick Cooper do?' Mick is clearly a very intelligent man who has engaged admirably with the world of counselling and psychotherapy research. He has been successful in publishing influential textbooks, important research papers and obtaining research funding. Each of these is no mean feat. In being successful Mick has put his head above the parapet and will have had to develop a relatively thick skin – in the world of academic research there will always be those who do not agree with what you stand up for. Furthermore, he will have had to juggle research deadlines alongside numerous other tasks associated with his academic role and personal life. It may therefore be understandable that either the criticism of his work or the numerous other tasks that he has to do could provide reason for him to throw in the towel and say enough is enough. So how do people overcome such challenges? Maybe the world of therapy has some potential answers. For instance, from a CBT perspective, challenging the negative thoughts behind the criticism might be one way of addressing the issues. Alternatively a person-centred therapist might examine the incongruence between the differing selves, or a psychodynamic practitioner might look at historical patterns of behaviour with significant others. Being realistic, we will not all be able to reach the same heady heights as researchers such as the aforementioned list of professors. We should, however, not forget the skills that we do have and how they might apply to our own lives. Whether we need to focus upon understanding our own self-criticism or just managing our time better to achieve our goals, therapy (or at least therapeutic skills) can be a useful way of us helping ourselves.

In relation to the final concern noted in our findings above, it is felt to be wholly appropriate that something of the researcher is shared in the work; it develops the epistemological position of the piece and strengthens the validity of conclusions reached. This is a strength of qualitative work in establishing its quality; such transparency, the need to be explicit, clear and open about the assumptions we make and the methods and procedures we use, is important in the presentation and dissemination of findings (Hiles, 2007). However, the reason for including such information must hold these issues at their core. There is always the danger that a piece of work can be narcissistic and navel gazing. If you do include reflective statements, make sure you always ask yourself the question 'so what?' Why have you written these thoughts into the work? Also, could your reflections sit alongside the writings of other authors?

I was keen to include an email to William in relation to this last point, so now let's have another musical interlude …

MUSICAL INTERLUDE 2

Hi William,
You asked me to write a few notes from what we were chatting about earlier, so these have been my thoughts about creative writing/writing style for the thesis/assignments – all inspired by fun with my baby grand piano!

So, music is made up of treble, alto, tenor and bass lines and each of these lines takes the theme at different times. Usually the sopranos in a choir will hold the main theme (treble), supported by harmonies from the other voice sections, but the main theme will often pass from voice part to voice part. Often it is most moving when the basses take over the main theme as their role is normally to offer harmonies to accompany the other voices. Sometimes too, one voice part is unaccompanied and this has a particular significance and beauty.

(Continued)

(Continued)

Anyway, it seems to me that writing can be thought of in a similar way. Imagine that the four voices in a thesis are:

theory/research/models (the academic/booky descriptive stuff)

the critical voice in relation to this material (strengths and weaknesses)

practice implications

personal reflections.

Write too much of one and you won't get a balanced thesis. Write an oratorio using just the sopranos and it will sound shrill and unsupported; add to it the resonance of some tenors and a few bass notes and you achieve a much fuller sound that shows off the beauty of the tune in the sopranos.

The point is: different parts of your writing will hold one, two, three or four voices in different combinations at different times. For example, the literature review is likely to be description and critical voice, perhaps with some elements of practice. Get to the discussion and you are likely to describe your themes and findings in relation to the theory, being critical of them but saying something of where they place themselves to you and your practice (all four voices potentially).

People often say to me, 'Where can I write *me* into the work?' It seems to me that anywhere is the answer, so long as you don't forget about the other voices in the writing. I get jumpy if I see one page of unreferenced writing because this implies to me it is just one voice – yours and that's fine (or you might be plagiarising!) but beware that you don't lose the other emphases that you need to produce a whole thesis. Could your own reflections be accompanied by the literature (so one voice becomes two), or even better supported by a critical review of the literature (three voices)?

Sometimes less is more and there will be times when you just want a solo to sing out in your work – but this won't work all the way through (i.e. you can't just write about your own processes and thoughts, much as you might want to!). Crashing chords all the way through a piece of music would not work either and could be confusing, but they will have their place; e.g. a thick and thorough discussion incorporating you, research, your findings and your practice is great.

The emphases will differ in your writing and that is good. Sometimes the tune will be helped by different voices, solo or accompanied.

I'm trying to think of a piece of music you could use to illustrate this. I'm thinking Verdi's Requiem, which is beautiful ….

Anyway, this is just what I have been thinking about for the last year or so. Feel free to use it if it makes some sense to you!

In conclusion to this section, a good piece of counselling research is likely to incorporate you, your practice and a critical review of the literature in relation to both method and topic.

Where might *your* research go?

So now that we have explored in previous chapters how you might establish a storyline to your research and the various voices that need to be contained within it, we will now consider the places that you might write for and the ways in which you could express your ideas given these differing audiences.

Writing for a qualification

The expectations of writing for a qualification can be greatly determined by the institution in which you are studying. There are however commonalities across courses that we feel can be summarised in a standard way. Within our work, we have adopted a relatively traditional house style and expect students to write within this framework unless there is good reason not to. This is not to say that it leads to 'samey' pieces of research. On the contrary, the fact that students know the 'shape' of the dissertation and the requirements of it enables individuals to think about how their research plans might be harnessed and held by such a structure. By using this house style we have been privileged to support some first-rate and courageous work.

Before you embark on a dissertation for a qualification, you will likely have been asked to write a research proposal, the main aims of which are to provide you with a 'map' of how you intend to get the final dissertation done. It is likely to use the same structure as the dissertation so that you can get an idea of the shape of the final piece and the chapters contained within it. For the dissertation there are four key points to remember (but also keep these in mind for the proposal):

1   Keep it simple.
2   Guide the reader by the hand throughout your work.
3   Make sure that the material that you cite is current, i.e. 2000+ where possible, although you will be including seminal pieces of work to rest the more contemporary research upon.
4   Be critical and questioning of the material you include and make sure that you justify the choices you make in terms of literature included and methodology adopted.

For the actual dissertation, and to a large extent the Doctoral thesis, the following provides an overview of each of the major chapters and what might be contained within them.

Abstract

To help you write this, imagine how you use someone else's abstract when you are researching. What are the things included in it that help you to decide on using the source any further? It is likely that it provides you with a summary of the aims, methods, results/findings and conclusions from the study and gives you a clear indication of what it is about. Increasingly, it is viewed as good practice actually to include these headings (or similar ones) in an abstract.

Introduction

This chapter is often used quite flexibly, but it sets the scene for the research study. Often the author will want to explain here why the problem they have chosen is one worth researching, and will describe it in relation to key indications from the literature and reflections or insights from practice that have resulted in the emergence of the questions to be explored. Essentially: what is it that you want to research and why? What is your main research question?

Literature review

This chapter is a review of the literature prior to you undertaking your work. What has gone on and what has been done? Set the scene for the reader so that they understand the academic context of your work. It is after this chapter that the piece becomes more 'you'; this chapter is the stage set before you enter the scene with your own research!

This chapter hinges on your research question holding the literature together. Think carefully about the key areas that you need to address – these will provide a structure to your work and often will also give key terms for a database search. What is more, the areas have emerged from your research question so you can be sure that they will help to 'hold' the report together. Try to structure your work so that it moves from the broad to the specific, like a funnel leading to a statement of your aims for the research and the question itself. The last section that you write should be those research papers that relate most closely to your question. If you find that there is nothing directly related to what you want to do, be prepared to look at the literature more generally related to your topic and explain that you have cited this material because there is a gap in this research area. Although scary, this provides a great rationale to your study.

Make sure that you are critical and provide a narrative to cement the various pieces of literature together. As though you were describing the chapter to your next-door neighbour, explain the relative merits of various pieces of research and then how your work develops these earlier findings. Do be critical and talk to us in a literature review – remember, your readers are human! A colleague of mine often says that he gets bored in literature reviews – you mustn't bore the marker! The first time I heard this I was aghast, partly because it goes against the mantra I was brought up on from my dad, that 'only boring people get bored' (although that's another story…), but as time has gone on I have certainly recognised the need to take this into account. I know that I found my literature review in my PhD the most tedious to read and I am sure it was because a lot of the time I wasn't sure what I was saying, so I wrote in a turgid, long-winded style.

Methodology

This chapter is more about you but also contains a literature review, this time in relation to methodology. Once again, it is probably best structured going from broad epistemological and methodological matters through to the procedures that you adopted in collecting your data. The idea is that this section should allow for replication by another researcher – clearly this is a complicated area in a qualitative study, but it is a useful benchmark to aim for in terms of your descriptions of what you did and particularly how you analysed the data. I have heard colleagues say that some qualitative methods of analysis are just about the researcher 'sitting there and thinking for a bit'. A good piece of qualitative research has particular strengths that can outwit a number-based project, but you need to justify your piece thoroughly so that it stands up to its audience.

You need also to consider here the ethical implications of your study and to embed it in an appropriate framework, otherwise it sounds as though you plucked your perfectly ethical practice from the sky.

This chapter should take us through from issues that you had to consider in deciding on your methods (i.e. methodological dilemmas), the methods adopted and ethical issues, right up to how you analysed the data, so that the next chapter can just hit the reader with what you found: your headlines.

Results/findings

In a quantitative piece this is the chapter where you provide the statistical findings of your research. The following chapter then discusses these findings, reiterating what you found in words. Clearly, in a more qualitative piece this decoding into words is unnecessary because you are dealing with words as your data. As you begin to outline your themes you might find that you want to relate the material back to the research in the literature review. This makes a lot of sense and results are sometimes combined with this discursive content in a chapter called something like 'Discussion of Findings'. You can of course elect to keep your findings separate – some people want to articulate clearly what they found in the 'Findings' chapter and then open out a new 'Discussion' chapter. Either is fine, but be sure and clear about what you have found. This sounds obvious, but I remember dreading people who asked me what I had 'found out' in my PhD! You need to work hard to articulate it clearly. Tables at the start of the chapter are useful, providing constant, clear signposts for the reader; a qualitative report can often be lengthy and by its very nature wordy!

Discussion

So, you have elected to present and discuss your findings together or separately. Either way, it is now your job to enter the conversation with the literature review. You are now part of the jigsaw and you need to explain how you fit. This might be taken one step further when you actually meet the authors that you cite at conference! You are legitimately there and you need to relate your findings with what has gone before. The picture has shifted slightly in the light of your undertaking this piece.

Conclusions

Clearly you also need to be humble in terms of your own research and, just as you talked about the strengths and weaknesses of other people's work, you need to do the same in your own. This section might be placed in the preceding discussion chapter.

You also need to consider, 'Where to next?' If someone else were to take up the baton, where could they go in terms of further research? Additionally, now is the time to consider what the point of this research is. What does it mean? What are its implications?

Although this section has given an overview of a 'classic' shape to a research project it is not meant to be prescriptive. It is however a useful 'container' to hold some interesting and creative thoughts. Awarding institutions seem to be quite keen on this sort of shape too.

Publication, conferences and beyond

If people have taken the trouble to participate in our research then I think we owe it to them to consider carefully the ways in which we disseminate the results. You might think that your findings are not that significant or important, or that you have done this work for an academic award and that is enough. However, even run-of-the-mill findings tell us something in our still under-researched world of counselling. It is likely that you will be the harshest critic of your work, so do check it out with someone else before you choose not to disseminate.

There are many ways of disseminating your research. First, tell your colleagues. This can be informally over coffee or it could be a presentation and/or brief report circulated via email or by paper. See what reactions you get.

The next step might be to consider presenting to a counselling audience you don't know. It's scary but most individuals have the skills, and if you have practised on your friends you will likely have learnt something from the exercise – for example less is usually more; a good picture or graphic tells a story better than 1,000 words; a joke usually helps, as does connecting the research to practice. Your training institution might well provide this next audience or certainly a source of useful suggestions.

Staying with presentations, the next step might be to apply to present at a national research conference such as the BACP Research Conference or BPS Counselling Psychology Conference. Both of these have their own way of doing things and you might need some guidance to avoid getting rejected. For instance, it might be that you have several options:

- **Present a poster:** This involves creating a poster summary of your work. This combines the challenge of making the research visually interesting with the need to make it appropriately concise. Posters are often perused by attendees during a coffee break and can be a great way to cut your teeth at attending conferences.
- **Present a paper:** This usually takes the format of a 20-minute presentation with 10 minutes of questions.
- **Present a paper within a symposium:** Some conferences attempt to put people into categories of similar research – e.g. school-based counselling research. These often take a similar format to the paper presentation noted above but involve three or four presentations in the one area. Questions might come at the end of the presentations.

Do check out the organisations' websites and talk to people who have been through the process before. Despite the initial challenge of getting involved, conferences are well worth attending, both to present at and, probably most importantly, to network with interested others. This step can then take you international. If you get a good reception nationally, then that week-long conference in Hawaii might become a reality.

If your nerve and enthusiasm get you to the presentation stage then you should definitely consider writing up your presentation as a paper for publication. This could be in professional publications such as *Therapy Today* or *The Psychologist*, or peer-reviewed research journals such as *Counselling and Psychotherapy Research, Counselling Psychology Review, Counselling Psychology Quarterly, The British Journal of Guidance and Counselling, The Journal of Critical Psychology Counselling and Psychotherapy* and so on. ('Peer review' means that people are invited to comment on the strengths and weakness of the work prior to publication – it is likely that this process will take some time and that you will have to respond to the comments of reviewers before publication – see Hanley and Steffen (2012) for an overview of this process.) All these journals have differing editorial lines, spoken and unspoken. It is probably not a good idea to write a paper and then think of where to send it; better to read around the journals and/or take advice, and then write with a particular journal in mind.

The printed paper is not the only form of dissemination and may well not be the best way to reach practitioners. Think of email lists or discussion groups you belong to or could join. Alternatively you might develop a new resource such as a website, blog or social network group – it takes a matter of minutes and often provides a free means to let people know about your research. If you feel very excited about the prospect of going multimedia you might record your presentation and upload it too – an avenue not for the faint-hearted!

To end this section it's important to link back to Chapter 5, in which we briefly reflect upon the impact of undertaking research. Within that chapter we mention that there could be fallout from going public with your research, both positive and negative. Do be prepared to field feedback from the work you set free into the world.

The student voice: Sue Dawson

Even in the absence of chocolate lips, strawberries and sparkling water, and without it being Valentine's Day, I must confess I am smitten, completely in love with research!!!! I enjoy thinking about research, ruminating on an idea, nurturing it to fruition. In exploring different methodologies for my research Doctorate in 2003 I came across Organic Inquiry (OI) (Curry and Wells, 2003), a methodology epistemologically situated within a transpersonal psychology paradigm that recognises the interconnected nature of being at multiple levels. OI is used with heuristic, phenomenological and narrative methods. It is frequently employed by practitioner psychologists and other therapists investigating more nebulous human experiences, including healing presence and liminal space between client and therapist, and intangible human experiences such as grief. OI places a premium on the transformative potential of research at multiple levels: within the self of the researcher, study participants and consumers of the research findings, effectively meaning that anyone at any stage coming into contact with research findings has the potential to be changed by them. Within OI *transformative change may be generated from feeling responses as well as cognition and reason.* As a narrative researcher, enabling others to bear witness to the lived experiences of grief of the participants in my PhD study (Dawson, 2007) was integral within the process, completion and presentation of the study findings. Bearing witness to the narratives of others generates new co-constructed narratives with new meanings from the research findings emerging; in this respect OI construes research findings as evolving and fluid through the process of intersubjective understanding. Talking about research and presenting findings in creative and multiple ways is pivotal to embracing the *transformative principle* within OI. No doubt this requirement further fuelled my passion for presenting my own research findings at different stages within the study in as many ways and to as many different communities as possible, including research participants (member checks, or what OI defines as resonance meetings), focus groups (described as resonance panels in OI), and academic, professional and lay communities. This chapter particularly grabbed my interest because of my belief in the transformative power of research and because of my passion for practitioner research, having seen how it has changed me as a person and a professional over the course of my counselling practice.

Whilst empirical evidence suggests that most of us in our therapeutic practice are less influenced by research than other factors, research has shaped the course of trajectory of my development as a counsellor – both my own research and coming into contact with others'. It is about thinking outside of the box. For me, consuming research is a true feast, but it is more than the written page and extends far beyond the thesis sitting on a dusty library shelf or in an academic journal article. Experiencing research findings first hand embodies knowledge in me and captures my own interest.

I remember meeting the narrative psychologist Bob Niemeyer for the first time in London, Ontario, at a conference at which I was presenting a paper on my preliminary PhD findings. He gave a workshop grounded in his most recent research but, animated and punctuated by the voice of lived experience, he used video footage of client work sensitively to illustrate findings and (most importantly for me) to privilege the voices of his study participants, or co-researchers as he described them. Bob Niemeyer works from a social constructionist perspective, perceiving knowledge as co-constructed; his workshop actively acknowledged this, inviting our perceptions and perspectives to generate new insights and co-create new knowledge. Similarly I attended a two-day workshop with Babette Rothschild introducing her research findings about the psychophysiology of compassion fatigue and vicarious trauma. We experienced the research findings in action through activities enabling embodied knowing. Both of these experiences significantly impacted on my practice and personal development. Yet as doctoral researchers we may shy away from offering workshops where our research studies can be situated within the context of current received wisdom and be open to critical peer scrutiny. In many respects presenting a seminar, workshop or poster can be more daunting for a researcher than giving a straight presentation, because of the interactive nature. I think it is all too easy to become protective and defensive of our research – it can become 'our baby' – but to grow to its full potential it is essential that it is nurtured through constant questioning, on-going critical evaluation and, most importantly, utilising the growth analogy from OI; as researchers we must be open to emergent new meanings generated by engagement with others – talking about our research is a dialectic process that enables growth. In many respects this critical community becomes the lifeblood that enables meaningful momentum in the research journey, nurturing new knowledge and facilitating potential for this knowledge to influence therapeutic practice.

As a narrative therapist and researcher, stories are central within my practice. Talking about research is for me a series of stories, and situating myself within the meta-narrative of the research is essential. With reflexivity comes an inherent danger of solipsism. Reflexivity is central within researcher transparency and I believe should be an integral component openly acknowledged within presentation of findings. Considering creative and expressive approaches to mapping reflexivity such as expressive artwork, sculpture or poetry can be useful in inviting engagement with research findings in different modalities. For art and expressive therapists these methods may sit particularly comfortably. Case studies can also be presented as stories or, as I did in my own research, a series of sequence poems, highlighted in different coloured text to illustrate consonance and dissonance between the different voices identified in analysis (voice-centred relational analysis). Whose voice has precedence in presenting research is a key ethical issue that should inform decisions about where to publish and present. Ensuring that participants' voices are heard for me is central within any aspect of talking about or presenting findings. Member checks and resonance panels are central to increasing trustworthiness of the findings; to be salient to our clients as well as practitioner colleagues, consideration should be given to publishing in popular magazines, making a website or writing a researcher blog. Enabling access for different consumers involves attention to how we write and the language used. Talking about research findings and responding to what we hear back, and learning from the criticisms made and the reflections of others, breathe continuous life into cycles of research and practice and real-world relevance.

Summary points

- Research crops up in all sorts of unexpected places – for example, conferences, corridors, pubs, books and journals. You are possibly more familiar with it than you think!
- It's important to be clear about the research question that you are writing your piece around. If you are not clear, the message of your research becomes muddled and you will find it hard to establish how it sits along the writings of other authors.
- Writing up research in this field is challenging as you have a number of voices to attend to: a critical review of the literature in relation to topic and methods, practice issues and personal reflection. Each of these voices will adopt a greater or lesser emphasis as appropriate in your work.
- There are major sections that you will need to write to for an academic paper or dissertation for a qualification.
- You need to get out there. Audiences are very diverse for counselling and psychotherapy research and you need to think carefully about the audience for whom you are writing regarding your pitch.

FURTHER READING

This final 'further reading' section provides no specific direction to texts on this subject matter. The reason for this is that we feel the best way to engage further with this topic is to create a more tailored response. This might include:

- finding research articles around topics that interest you
- writing a research paper about a piece of research you have undertaken
- going to a research conference
- presenting at a research conference
- discussing research findings with colleagues – formally or informally.

Such activities will help to consolidate many of the concepts discussed throughout this chapter.

10

Summary

Overview

This chapter strays from the format of modelling research terminology at the outset. As is evident from the above title, it begins with an overview rather than an abstract. The purpose of straying away from our strategy revolves around the format adopted below. In bringing the subject matter of this text together, rather than summarise the sections in turn, we present an overview of the work in the traditional format of a research paper. Here we attempt to weave together the key points made throughout the text and outline how this text itself could be framed as a research endeavour. (Please note that the data presented in this component is completely fictional.) Finally, to end the book, we present three final thoughts related to the completion of writing.

THOUGHT BOX 10

How might you view this book as a piece of research?

Consider:

- What type of research question might you pose?
- Why might your project be important to the profession?
- What considerations might you have when preparing to undertake the project?
- How might you anticipate the project impacting upon you?
- What type of data might you be able to generate?
- How might you analyse this data?
- What ethical issues might you consider?
- How might you distribute your research project?

Abstract

Background: Counsellors and psychotherapists are becoming increasingly mindful of the impact that research is having upon their work. Despite this there is limited evidence to suggest that research findings play a significant role in influencing individuals' therapeutic practice. *Methodology:* A mixed methods research design has been adopted to explore a) the success of a series of training activities in raising research awareness, and b) the strengths and challenges associated with these activities. Goal-based outcomes are examined alongside standardised outcome scores and satisfaction ratings. The quantitative data is analysed for relationships between the different factors (goals × outcomes × satisfaction). Such findings are then explained through use of the qualitative data. This is analysed using grounded theory. *Findings:* The findings are idiosyncratic in nature and vary from individual to individual. *Discussion:* The discussion that surrounds the success of the activities in this text echoes those that occur within therapeutic discourses. In particular, self-identified goals need not relate directly to more standardised expectations or overall satisfaction ratings. Furthermore, the qualitative findings help to explain why this proves to be the case.

Key words

Counselling, psychotherapy, research, training activities, mixed methods

Background

Encouraging counsellors and psychotherapists to become more informed consumers of research has become an increasingly important agenda for this profession (as indicated in Chapter 2). In particular, the fear that the profession is not able to justify its own existence using high-quality systematic research (see Chapter 3 for more on this), or defend established practices using the bodies of research available, has led therapeutic organisations to heighten the importance of research within training curricula.

The move to raise the profile of research in the counselling and psychotherapy professions has received mixed blessings. There are those who wholeheartedly back this agenda and there are also those who struggle to see the relevance that research plays within therapeutic practice. The negative views can often be accompanied by the challenges of engaging and undertaking research (as discussed in Chapters 4 and 5).

Despite the increased agenda to develop a more research-informed profession, little research has been undertaken to examine how this might occur. The lack of research in this area therefore leads to the need for a more systematic investigation into the way that training activities can facilitate counsellors' and psychotherapists' engagement with research. The project reported here does just that and reflects upon the way in which therapists develop their research skills whilst reading an introductory research text directed at counsellors and psychotherapists.

Research questions

Two major research questions are asked within this research project. These are noted below with their associated sub-questions:

RQ1: Can research awareness be increased by the contents of an introductory research text directed at counsellors and psychotherapists?

- Is this achieved to a degree in which the reader is satisfied by their developments?
- Are the reader's self-identified goals met by the content of the book?
- Can changes in the reader's research awareness be observed using a standardised set of questions?

The second question focuses more on the qualitative engagement with the text. This aims to explain the numbers generated from RQ1 and is as follows:

RQ2: What strengths and weaknesses do readers identify whilst reading this book?

Methodology

An explanatory mixed methods design combining both quantitative and qualitative research methods has been used within this piece of work. Specifically, the qualitative data that has been generated aims to complement and explain the findings from the quantitative component (see Chapters 6 and 7 for information about quantitative and qualitative research. Also see Chapter 6 for an introduction to mixed methods research).

Participants

The major participants in this study were the individuals reading through the text. Their inclusion in the project was determined by their engagement with the content of the text and the activities within it.

So as to be transparent about the design of the study, it is also important to comment upon the researchers in the project. The three individuals involved in this project are counselling trainers who have an interest in teaching research methods to therapists. They are the authors of the activities and thus cautious about the impact their biases may have upon the work.

Research design

This project has four major components. These are outlined in turn as follows:

1 Satisfaction

Each individual, on reaching the end of the book, has been asked how satisfied they have been with the contents of the book. This is a simple descriptive statistic rated on a six-point Likert scale (0 being 'not at all' and 5 being 'completely').

2 Goal-based outcomes

The goals that individuals set at the start of the textbook are reflected upon to see how well they were met now that the reader has reached the end of the book. As with the satisfaction component to the evaluation, each goal is rated on a six-point Likert scale with 0 indicating that the goal has not been attained and 5 indicating that it has been completely attained.

3 Standardised measure

This component uses the SARA scale (see Chapter 1 for more about the development of this tool). This self-report questionnaire asked respondents to rate their knowledge of eight research topics using a standard set of statements (0 = I know nothing about this, 5 = I am very aware of this issue). These topics were:

- The research that underpins therapy
- What is the purpose of research?
- The issues related to preparing to undertake research
- The impact that research has upon the researcher
- Quantitative research
- Qualitative research
- The ethical issues within therapy research
- The arenas in which counselling and psychotherapy research is talked about

4 Qualitative information

The final element of this evaluation is qualitative in nature and aimed to explain the scores that have been indicated above. Individuals were invited to write a brief statement about the strengths and weaknesses that they perceived in the textbook being examined.

Data analysis

As with the data generation section above, it is necessary for us to outline the methods of data analysis for the four strands of the research. Once again these are considered in turn.

1 Satisfaction

The data generated from the six-point scale automatically provides insight into how satisfied the reader has been with the text. This can be summarised on its own and potentially compared with the scores of others.

2 Goal-based outcomes

The statements identifying the goals of the participant have been monitored at two points. Following the identification of the reader's goals within the introductory chapter, the first review reflected upon the completion of these goals at a mid-point in the book (within Chapter 6). This is then compared with those reported at the completion of the text. The data generated at these stages are compared with each other for differences in the scores. Additionally, the total change indicated using this tool is reported as a mean average (see Chapter 6 for further details about quantitative data analysis).

3 Standardised measures

As with the goal-based outcome data this information is used alongside data collected at several stages in the book. These stages are: 1) at the outset of the book; 2) at a mid-point in the book; 3) at the end of the book. The different topics are considered individually and as a whole. Specifically they are summarised as mean scores rated from 0 to 5.

4 Qualitative information

All of the qualitative data that is generated has been analysed using grounded theory techniques (see Chapter 7 for a brief overview of qualitative data analysis). This has involved breaking the text down into small meaning units before examining the data for commonalities. These commonalities have then been pulled together into larger themes (axial codes) and a core category that harnesses all of the discussions created. Credibility checks, in the form of a member check (see the 'Student Voice' sections of the text for examples of this type of method), have been used within the work. Respondents were asked to consider the accuracy of their summary of the text and invited to revise it if necessary.

Ethical considerations

The authors are either accredited members of the BACP (WW) or HCPC-registered Practitioner Psychologists and Chartered Counselling Psychologists with the BPS (TH and CL). With this in mind, all of the work presented here adheres to the ethical frameworks of these professional bodies (BACP, 2010; BPS, 2009; HCPC, 2008). In particular, we would note that each activity was outlined clearly so that participants could provide informed consent to participate. Furthermore, the autonomous nature of the tasks undertaken in this book enabled participants to withdraw at any point in time (see Chapter 8 for more about ethical considerations in research).

Findings

This section requires each individual reader to fill in the gaps to reflect their experience of reading the book. In particular the sections noted in square brackets require the reader to insert their own meanings. In contemplating what this may look like we will discuss each question in turn.

1 Satisfaction

Satisfaction with the text was rated as [enter your number from 0–5] out of five. This indicated that the reader was not at all satisfied/moderately satisfied/very satisfied [delete as appropriate] with the content of the book.

2 Goal-based outcomes

Three goals were identified at the outset of this text – these were [insert goals here]. Table 5 summarises the goal-based outcome scores. These are graphically represented in Graphs 6, 7 and 8.

Table 5 A summary of the goal-based outcome data

Goal	Mid-way score	Post score	Change
1	1	5	+4
2	3	3	0
3	5	1	−4

Graph 6   A summary of scores for Goal 1

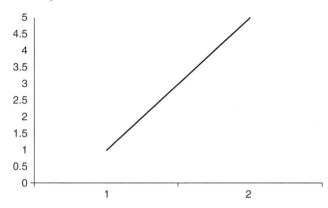

Graph 7   A summary of scores for Goal 2

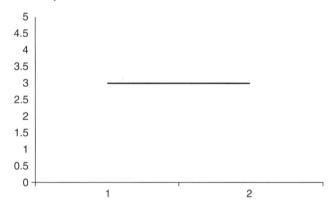

Graph 8   A summary of scores for Goal 3

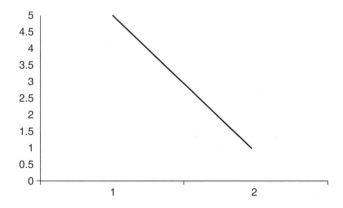

3 Standardised measures

This section briefly summarises the SARA scores for an individual reading the textbook. Table 6 provides a summary of this data. Graphs 9 and 10 also summarise the scores, with Graph 9 providing a summary of the individual questions and Graph 10 providing a summary of the mean score of all components of the questionnaire.

Table 6 A summary of the SARA data

Question	Pre score	Mid score	Post score
1	1	5	5
2	3	3	3
3	5	3	1
4	0	2	2
5	5	5	5
6	2	2	3
7	5	5	5
8	4	2	1
Mean	3.125	3.375	3.125

Graph 9 A summary of individual SARA scores at three intervals

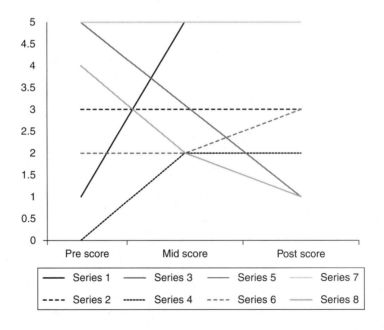

Graph 10 A summary of cumulative SARA scores at three intervals

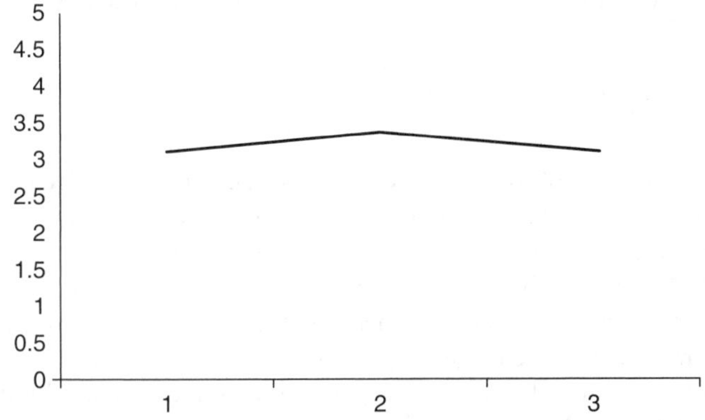

4 Qualitative information

The qualitative data that was generated was analysed using grounded theory. From this process the core category of '[insert theme]' was elicited. Subsumed within this were four major themes (axial codes). These were: 1) [insert theme]; 2) [insert theme]; 3) [insert theme]; 4) [insert theme]. Table 7 summarises these themes and provides a summary of the number of times they were mentioned within the transcript.

Table 7 A summary of the major themes elicited from the grounded theory analysis

Theme	Number of mentions
1 Writing style	7
2 Content	20
3 Activities	9
4 Etc.	...

Below we will introduce each of these and provide illustrative quotes grounded within the data.

[Insert description of each theme alongside illustrative quotes].

Discussion

Two research questions were posed in this study. The way in which the findings of this project relate to these questions is briefly answered here. Additionally, the way in which the different data sets interact is discussed, with the qualitative data working to explain the quantitative data. Throughout, the findings are related back to the original literature presented at the outset of this paper.

[We have to allow you to fill in the gap related to your findings here.]

Limitations and future studies

This is a small-scale piece of work in which we have generated a detailed overview of one person's experience of engaging with an introductory research text for counsellors and psychotherapists. It would be very helpful to explore this further with a wider selection of individuals. It would also be important to consider the influence of other factors upon individuals' learning processes. For instance, the impact of training programmes is also likely to have influenced any change in reported competence.

In relation to the above limitation, further work should explore the impact of the text in question on a wider number of individuals. In doing so, it would be helpful to consider the impact of the text in relation to those that were, and were not, supported by alternative means (e.g. additional introductory research texts or research programmes). It may also be helpful to consider utilising externally reported data, rather than self-report data. Such data would allow for some comparison when considering the impact of the text upon how research informed individuals are.

The qualitative data highlighted numerous areas for improvement within the text. This has been vital in improving the overall package on offer. It is recommended that any future evaluations account for these changes.

Final thought 1: Keep engaging with research

As advocated in Chapter 9 of this text, we hope that you continue your discussions about counselling and psychotherapy research. In continuing the discussions we hope that you see research becoming a part of your everyday practice (if it were not already) and that you consider taking part in extra-curricular research activities. For instance, maybe we will meet you at a research conference, read one of your articles or attend a presentation that you are making. Additionally, please use this book as a vehicle for continuing your discussions. Be critical and consider what we have done well and what you feel we have not achieved. Check out your views with colleagues or friends (as we have with our trainees here) and have a dialogue about its contents. Such engaged reflections will help to develop your own academic voice.

Final thought 2: Trying to embrace the inevitable disappointment

All three of us sat down at the end of the writing of this book to reflect upon the achievement of finishing it. Despite the sense of relief that goes with finishing a large task such as this, it was clear that each of us was also a little disappointed. So why was that? Unfortunately, from our perspective, the reality of any long writing project (book, paper, thesis, dissertation, report, etc.) is that you are in a better position to write the thing when you have finished than when you started. Churning over the topic, no matter how familiar you are with it in the first instance, helps to synthesise your understanding of it. In this instance, we had numerous meetings and writing sessions, edited the content and so on, and learnt from it. In the aforementioned celebratory meeting, because of this we sat down and pulled out the weaknesses in the text and considered what we would do if we were to rewrite it afresh. It was, however, time for us to let go of the manuscript and let it develop a life of its own in relation with others.

Final thought 3: Thank you

We hope that now you have come to the end of our book, the content in the fictional paper noted above makes sense. More importantly we hope that you have enjoyed our writing and found it useful in the work that you are doing. Thank you.

References

Adams, D. (1979) *The Hitchhiker's Guide to the Galaxy*. London: Pan.

Ankrah, L. (2000) 'Experiences of dealing with spiritual emergencies within counselling relationships'. MA in Counselling Studies dissertation, University of Manchester, Manchester.

Asay, T. and Lambert, M. (2000) 'The empirical case for the common factors in therapy: quantitative findings', in M. Hubble, B. Duncan and S. Miller (eds), *The Heart and Soul of Change: What Works in Therapy*. Washington, DC: American Psychological Association.

Barkham, M. (2003) 'Quantitative research on psychotherapeutic interventions: methods and findings across four research generations', in R. Woolfe, W. Dryden and S. Strawbridge (eds), *Handbook of Counselling Psychology*, Second Edition. London: Sage.

Beck A., Ward C. and Mendelson, M. (1961) 'An inventory for measuring depression', *Arch. Gen. Psychiatry*, 4: 561–71.

Bergin, A.E. and Garfield, S.L. (eds) (1994) *Handbook of Psychotherapy and Behavior Change*. New York: Wiley.

Blackburn, I.M., James, I.A., Milne, D.L. and Reichelt, F.K. (2001) 'The revised cognitive therapy scale (CTSR): psychometric properties', *Behavioural and Cognitive Psychotherapy*, 29: 431–47.

Blair, L. (2010) 'A critical review of the scientist-practitioner model for counselling psychology', *Counselling Psychology Review*, 25 (4): 19–30.

Bloor, M., Frankland, J., Thomas, M. and Robson, K. (2001) *Focus Groups in Social Research*. London: Sage.

Bohart, A.C. (2005) 'Evidence-based psychotherapy means evidence-informed, not evidence-driven', *Journal of Contemporary Psychotherapy*, 35 (1): 39–53.

Bond, T. (2000) *Standards and Ethics for Counselling in Action*, Second Edition. London: Sage.

Bond, T. (2004) 'Ethical guidelines for researching counselling and psychotherapy', *Counselling and Psychotherapy Research*, 4 (2): 10–19.

Braun, V. and Clarke, V. (2006) 'Using thematic analysis in psychology', *Qualitative Research in Psychology*, 20 (3): 77–101.

Bretherton, I. (1992) 'The origins of attachment theory: John Bowlby and Mary Ainsworth', *Developmental Psychology*, 28 (5): 759–75.

BACP (British Association for Counselling and Psychotherapy) (2010) *Ethical Framework for Good Practice in Counselling and Psychotherapy*. Leicestershire: BACP.

BPS (British Psychological Society) (2009) *Code of Ethics and Conduct*. Leicester: BPS.

BPS (British Psychological Society) (2010) *Code of Human Research Ethics*. Leicester: BPS.

Christodoulidi, F. (2006) 'Spirituality and culture in counselling and psychotherapy: practitioners' perspectives'. MSc in Educational Research dissertation, University of Manchester, Manchester.

Clark D., Fairburn, C. and Wessely, S. (2008) 'Psychological treatment outcomes in routine NHS services: a commentary on Stiles et al (2007)', *Psychological Medicine*, 38: 629–34.

Cloke, P., Cooke, J., Cursons, P. and Milbourne, R. (2000) 'Ethics, reflexivity and research: encounters with homeless people', *Ethics, Place and Environment*, 3 (2): 133–5.

Cooper, M. (2008) *Essential Research Findings in Counselling and Psychotherapy: The Facts are Friendly*. London: Sage.

Cooper, M. (2009) 'Counselling in UK secondary schools: a comprehensive review of audit and evaluation data', *Counselling and Psychotherapy Research*, 9 (3): 137–50.

Cooper, M. and McLeod, J. (2010) *Pluralistic Counselling and Psychotherapy*. London: Sage.

Corbin, J. and Strauss, A. (2008) *Basics of Qualitative Research: Techniques and Procedures for Developing Grounded Theory*. London: Sage.

Cormack, J. (2009) 'Counselling marginalised young people: a qualitative analysis of young homeless people's views of counselling', *Counselling and Psychotherapy Research*, 9 (2): 71–7.

Creswell, J. (2003) *Research Design: Qualitative, Quantitative and Mixed Methods Approaches*, Second Edition. London: Sage.

Creswell, J. and Plano-Clark, V. (2010) *Designing and Conducting Mixed Methods Research*, Second Edition. London: Sage.

Curry, D. and Wells, S.J. (2003) *An Organic Inquiry Primer for the Novice Researcher*. Seattle: Liminal Realities.

Dallos, R. and Vetere, A. (2005) *Researching Psychotherapy and Counselling*. Maidenhead: Open University Press.

Dawson, S.E. (2007) 'Companion animal euthanasia: the lived paradox of the human-companion animal bond'. Unpublished Doctoral thesis, School of Psychology, Health and Social Care, Manchester Metropolitan University, Manchester.

Douglas, B.G. and Moustakas, C. (1985) 'Heuristic enquiry: the internal search to know', *Journal of Humanistic Inquiry*, 25 (3): 39–45.

Duncan, B., Miller, S., Wampold, B. and Hubble, M. (2010) *Heart and Soul of Change: Delivering What Works in Therapy*, Second Edition. Washington: APA.

Dyer, C., Joseph, S. and Coolican, H. (2005) 'Dealing with paired datasets: graphical and statistical approaches', *Counselling and Psychotherapy Research*, 5 (4): 256–7.

Elliott, R., Fischer, C.T. and Rennie, D.L. (1999) 'Evolving guidelines for the publication of qualitative research studies in psychology and related fields', *British Journal of Clinical Psychology*, 38: 215–29.

Elliott, R., Freire, B. and Westwell, G. (2011) 'The Person-Centred and Experiential Psychotherapy Scale (PCEPS): an introduction'. Presentation at the British Association for Counselling and Psychotherapy Annual Research Conference, Glasgow, May 2011.

Etherington, K. (2004) *Becoming a Reflexive Researcher: Using Our Selves in Research*. London: Jessica Kingsley Publishers.

Eysenck, H. (1952) 'The effects of psychotherapy', in H. Eysenck (ed.), *Handbook of Abnormal Psychology*. New York: Basic Books.

Feinstein, A.R. (1995) 'Meta-analysis: statistical alchemy for the 21st century', *Journal of Clinical Epidemiology*, 48: 71–9.

Feltham, C. (2010) *Critical Thinking in Counselling and Psychotherapy*. London: Sage.

Field, A. (2009) *Discovering Statistics Using SPSS*, Third Edition. London: Sage.

Frank, J. (1961) *Persuasion and Healing*. Baltimore: Johns Hopkins University Press.

French, T. (1933) 'Interrelations between psychoanalysis and the experimental work of Pavlov', *American Journal of Psychiatry*, 14: 239–45.

Freud, S. (1901/1990) 'The case of Dora', *Pelican Freud Library, Vol. 8: Case Histories 1*. Harmondsworth: Penguin.

Galton, F. (1863) *Meteorographica, or, Methods of Mapping the Weather*. London: Macmillan.

Ghaemi, A. (2009) *A Clinician's Guide to Statistics and Epidemiology in Mental Health: Measuring Truth and Uncertainty*. Cambridge: Cambridge University Press.

Gibbard, I. and Hanley, T. (2008) 'An evaluation of the effectiveness of person centred counselling in routine clinical practice in primary care', *Counselling and Psychotherapy Research*, 8 (4): 215–22.

Glaser, B. and Strauss, A. (1967) *The Discovery of Grounded Theory*. Chicago: Aldine.

Goldacre, B. (2008) *Bad Science*. London: Fourth Estate.

Goodwin, I., Holmes, G., Cochrane, R. and Mason, O. (2003) 'The ability of adult mental health services to meet clients' attachment needs: the development and implementation of the Service Attachment Questionnaire', *Psychology and Psychotherapy: Theory , Research and Practice*, 76 (2): 145–61.

Goss, S. and Mearns, D. (1997a) 'A call for a pluralist epistemological understanding in the assessment and evaluation of counselling', *British Journal of Guidance and Counselling*, 25 (2): 189–98.

Goss, S. and Mearns, D. (1997b) 'Applied pluralism in the evaluation of employee counselling', *British Journal of Guidance and Counselling*, 25 (3): 327–44.

Guba, E. and Lincoln, Y. (1994) 'Competing paradigms in qualitative research', in N. Denzin and Y. Lincoln (eds), *Handbook of Qualitative Research*. Thousand Oaks: Sage.

Hammersley, M. (2009) 'Against the ethicists: on the evils of ethical regulation', *International Journal of Social Research Methodology*, 12 (3): 211–25.

Hanley, T. (2009) 'The working alliance in online therapy with young people: preliminary findings', *British Journal of Guidance and Counselling*, 37 (3): 257–69.

Hanley, T. (2012) 'Understanding the online therapeutic alliance through the eyes of adolescent service users', *Counselling and Psychotherapy Research*, 12 (1): 35–43.

Hanley, T. and Lennie, C. (2008) 'Setting up a student research group', *The Psychologist*, 21 (2): 129.

Hanley, T. and Steffen, E. (2012) 'Writing for publication', *Counselling Psychology Review*, 21 (3): 3–10.

Hanley, T., Cutts, L., Gordon, R. and Scott, A. (2012) 'A research informed approach to counselling psychology', in G. Davey (ed.), *Applied Psychology*. Chichester: BPS Wiley Blackwell.

HCPC (Health and Care Professions Council) (2008) *Standards of Conduct, Performance and Ethics*. London: HCPC.

Hiles, D.R. (2007) 'Identity positioning: narrative analysis of Sjuzet and Fabula', in D. Robinson, N. Kelly and K. Milnes (eds), *Narrative and Memory*. Huddersfield: University of Huddersfield Press.

Hill, C. and Williams, E. (2000) 'The process of individual therapy', in S.D. Brown and R.W. Lent (eds), *Handbook of Counseling Psychology*, Third Edition. New York: Wiley.

Hollanders, H. (2000) 'Eclecticism/integration: historical developments', in S. Palmer and R. Woolfe (eds), *Integrative and Eclectic Counseling and Psychotherapy*. London: Sage.

James, G. (2004) 'In counselling, are there particular difficulties for clients with Christian beliefs around bereavement issues?' MA in Counselling Studies dissertation, University of Manchester, Manchester.

Johnson, R. and Onwuegbuzie, A. (2004) 'Mixed methods: a research paradigm whose time has come', *Educational Researcher*, 33 (7): 14–26.

Joseph, S., Dyer, C. and Coolican, H. (2005a) 'Means and standard deviations explained', *Counselling and Psychotherapy Research*, 5 (3): 256–7.

Joseph, S., Dyer, C. and Coolican, H. (2005b) 'What does p < .05 mean?', *Counselling and Psychotherapy Research*, 5 (2): 105–6.

Karasu, T. (1986) 'The specificity versus nonspecificity dilemma: toward identifying therapeutic change agents', *American Journal of Psychiatry*, 143: 687–95.

Kvale, S. and Brinkmann, S. (2009) *InterViews: Learning the Craft of Qualitative Research Interviewing*, Second Edition. London: Sage.

Lambert, M. (ed.) (2004) *Bergin and Garfield's Handbook of Psychotherapy and Behavior Change*, Fifth Edition. New York: Wiley.

Lambert, M. (2011) *Prevention of Treatment Failure: The Use of Measuring, Monitoring, and Feedback in Clinical Practice*. Washington: APA.

Lambert, M. and Barley, D. (2002) 'Research summary on the therapeutic relationship and psychotherapy outcome', in J. Norcross (ed.), *Psychotherapy Relationships that Work: Therapist Contributions and Responsiveness to Patients*. Oxford: Oxford University Press.

Lambert, M. and Bergin, A. (1994) 'The effectiveness of psychotherapy', in A. Bergin and S. Garfield (eds), *Handbook of Psychotherapy and Behavior Change*, Fourth Edition. New York: Wiley.

Lemma, A., Roth, A. and Pilling, S. (2008) *The Competences Required to Deliver Effective Psychoanalytic/Psychodynamic Therapy*. London: University College London.

Lennie, C. (2007) 'The role of personal development groups in counsellor training: understanding factors contributing to self-awareness in the personal development group', *British Journal of Guidance and Counselling*, 35 (1): 115–29.

Lennie, C. and West, W. (2010) 'Dilemmas in counselling psychology research', *Counselling Psychology Quarterly*, 23 (1): 83–9.

Longmore, R.J. and Worrell, M. (2007) 'Do we need to challenge thoughts in cognitive behavior therapy?', *Clinical Psychology Review*, 27: 173–87.

Lowndes, L. and Hanley, T. (2010) 'The challenge of becoming an integrative counsellor: the trainee's perspective', *Counselling and Psychotherapy Research*, 10 (3): 163–72.

Luborsky, L., Singer, B. and Luborsky, L. (1975) 'Comparative studies of psychotherapies: "Is it true that everybody has won and all must have prizes?"', *Archives of General Psychiatry*, 32: 995–1008.

Mair, D. (2003) 'Gay men's experiences of therapy', *Counselling and Psychotherapy Research*, 3 (1): 33–41.

Mansell W. (2008) 'What is CBT really and how can we enhance the impact of effective psychotherapies such as CBT?', in R. House and D. Loewenthal (eds), *Against and For CBT: Towards a Constructive Dialogue*. Ross-on-Wye: PCCS Books.

Mansell, W. and Taylor, J. (2012) 'What is CBT?', in W. Dryden (ed.), *The CBT Handbook*. London: Sage.

Matthews, B. and Ross, L. (2010) *Research Methods: A Practical Guide for the Social Sciences*. Oxford: Pearson Education.

May, R. (1975) *The Courage to Create*. London: Norton.

McLeod, J. (2003) *Doing Counselling Research*, Second Edition. London: Sage.

McLeod, J. (2009) *An Introduction to Counselling*, Fourth Edition. Maidenhead: Open University Press.

McLeod, J. (2010) *Case Study Research in Counselling and Psychotherapy*. London: Sage.

McLeod, J. (2011) *Qualitative Research in Counselling and Psychotherapy*, Second Edition. London: Sage.

Morgan, D. (2007) 'Paradigms lost and pragmatism regained: methodological implications of combining qualitative and quantitative methods', *Journal of Mixed Methods Research*, 1 (1): 48–76.

Morrow-Bradley, C. and Elliott, R. (1986) 'Utilization of psychotherapy research by practicing psychotherapists', *American Psychologist*, 41: 188–97.

Moustakas, C. (1990) *Heuristic Research: Design, Methodology and Applications*. London: Sage.

National Commission for the Protection of Biomedical and Behavioural Research (1978) *Institutional Review Boards*. Washington, DC: DHEW Government Printing Office.

Norcross, J. (ed.) (2011) *Psychotherapy Relationships that Work: Evidence-based Responsiveness*, Second Edition. Oxford: Oxford University Press.

Orlinsky, D.E., Botermans, J.-F., Rønnestad, M.H. and SPR Collaborative Network (2001) 'Towards an empirically grounded model of psychotherapy training: four thousand therapists rate influences on their development', *Australian Psychologist*, 36: 139–48.

Pixton, S. (2002) 'Experiencing gay affirmative therapy: an exploration of clients' views of what is helpful'. MA in Counselling Studies dissertation, University of Manchester, Manchester.

Polanyi, M. (1962) *Personal Knowledge*. Chicago: University of Chicago Press.

Rennie, D.L. (1994) 'Qualitative analysis of the client's experience of psychotherapy: the unfolding of reflexivity', in S.G. Toukmanian and D.L. Rennie (eds), *Psychotherapy Process Research: Paradigmatic and Narrative Approaches*. Newbury Park: Sage.

Research Assessment Exercise (2005) *RAE 2008: Guidance on Submissions*. Bristol: HEFCE.

Rogers, C. (1985) 'Towards a more human science of the person', *Journal of Humanistic Psychology*, 25 (4): 7–24.

Rosenzweig, S. (1936) 'Some implicit common factors in diverse methods in psychotherapy', *American Journal of Orthopsychiatry*, 6: 412–15.

Roth, A. and Pilling, S. (2007) *The Competences Required to Deliver Effective Cognitive and Behavioural Therapy for People with Depression and with Anxiety Disorders*. London: Department of Health.

Roth, A., Hill, A. and Pilling, S. (2009) *The Competences Required to Deliver Effective Humanistic Psychological Therapies.* London: University College London.

Rozin, P. (2001) 'Social psychology and science: some lessons from Solomon Asch', *Personality and Social Psychology Review,* 5 (1): 2–14.

Sackett, D.L. (1996) 'Levels of evidence and clinical decision making', in J. Basmajian and S. Banerjee (eds), *Clinical Decision Making in Rehabilitation: Efficacy and Outcomes.* New York: Churchill Livingstone.

Sanders, P. and Wilkins, P. (2010) *First Steps in Practitioner Research: A Guide to Understanding and Doing Research in Counselling and Health and Social Care.* Ross-on-Wye: PCCS Books.

Saunders, L. (2003) 'On flying, writing poetry and doing educational research', *British Educational Research Journal,* 29 (2): 175–87.

Schön, D. (1987) *Educating the Reflective Practitioner.* San Francisco: Jossey-Bass.

Scott, A. (2008) 'The effect of doing qualitative research on novice researchers', *European Journal for Qualitative Research in Psychotherapy,* 3: 10–18.

Silvester, A. (2011) 'Doing a Doc! The thoughts, experiences and relationships of students undertaking a Professional Doctorate in Counselling', *Counselling and Psychotherapy Research,* 11 (3): 179–85.

Smith, J., Flowers, P. and Larkin, M. (2009) *Interpretative Phenomenological Analysis: Theory, Method and Research.* London: Sage.

Smith, M. and Glass, G. (1977) 'Meta-analysis of psychotherapy outcome studies', *American Psychologist,* 32: 752–60.

Somekh, B. and Lewin, C. (2005) *Research Methods in the Social Sciences.* London: Sage.

Speedy, J. (2008) *Narrative Inquiry and Psychotherapy.* London: Palgrave.

Stoltenberg, C.D., Pace, T.M., Kashubeck, W.S., Biever, J.L., Patterson, T. and Welch, I.D. (2000) 'Training models in counseling psychology: scientist-practitioner versus practitioner-scholar', *Counseling Psychologist,* 28: 622–40.

Strawbridge, S. and Woolfe, R. (2010) 'Counselling psychology: origins, developments and challenges', in R. Woolfe, S. Strawbridge, B. Douglas and W. Dryden (eds), *Handbook of Counselling Psychology,* Third Edition. London: Sage.

Timulak, L. (2008) *Research in Psychotherapy and Counselling.* London: Sage.

Twenge, J.M. (2009) 'The jury's still out, but it might be decreasing', *American Psychologist,* 64 (1): 28–31.

Twigg, E., Barkham, M., Bewick, B., Mulhern, B., Connell, J. and Cooper, M. (2009) 'The Young Person's CORE: development of a brief outcome measure for young people', *Counselling and Psychotherapy Research,* 9 (3): 160–8.

Walker, T. (2009) '"Seeing beyond the battled body." An insight into selfhood and identity from women's accounts who self-harm with a diagnosis of borderline personality disorder', *Counselling and Psychotherapy Research,* 22: 122–8.

Wampold, B. (2001a) 'Contextualizing psychotherapy as a healing practice: culture, history and methods', *Applied and Preventive Psychology,* 10: 69–86.

Wampold, B. (2001b) *The Great Psychotherapy Debate: Models, Methods, and Findings.* Hillsdale, NJ: Lawrence Erlbaum Associates.

Watson, G. (1940) 'Areas of agreement in psychotherapy', *American Journal of Orthopsychiatry*, 10: 698–709.

Watson, J.B. and Rayner, R. (1920) 'Conditioned emotional reactions', *Journal of Experimental Psychology*, 3: 1–14.

West, W. (1997) 'Integrating counselling, psychotherapy and healing: an inquiry into counsellors and psychotherapist whose work includes healing', *British Journal of Guidance and Counselling*, 25 (3): 291–312.

West, W. (1998) 'Developing practice in a context for religious faith: a study of psychotherapists who are Quakers', *British Journal of Guidance and Counselling*, 26 (3): 365–75.

West, W. (2002) 'Some ethical dilemmas in counselling and counselling', *British Journal of Guidance and Counselling*, 30 (3): 261–8.

West, W. (2009) 'Situating the researcher in qualitative psychotherapy research around spirituality', *Counselling Psychology Quarterly*, 22 (2): 187–95.

West, W. (2011) 'Using the tacit dimension in qualitative research in counselling psychology', *Counselling Psychology Review*, 26 (4): 40–5.

West, W. and Hanley, T. (2006) 'Technically incompetent or generally misguided: learning from a failed counselling research project', *Counselling and Psychotherapy Research*, 6 (3): 209–12.

Westen, D., Novotny, C.M. and Thompson-Brenner, H. (2004) 'The empirical status of empirically supported psychotherapies: assumptions, findings, and reporting in controlled clinical trials', *Psychological Bulletin*, 130 (4): 631–63.

Wheeler, S. and Elliott, R. (2008) 'What do counsellors and psychotherapists need to know about research?', *Counselling and Psychotherapy Research*, 8 (2): 133–5.

Williams, G. (2010) 'The role of creativity in transformation and healing: an inquiry'. MA in Counselling Studies dissertation, University of Manchester, Manchester.

Index